THE SECRET MARATHON

THE SECRET MARATHON

EMPOWERING WOMEN AND GIRLS IN AFGHANISTAN THROUGH SPORT

MARTIN PARNELL

RMB

Other books by Martin Parnell

Marathon Quest

Running to the Edge

RMB | Rocky Mountain Books Ltd.
rmbooks.com
@rmbooks
facebook.com/rmbooks

Cataloguing data available from Library and Archives Canada
ISBN 9781771602990 (paperback)
ISBN 9781771603003 (electronic)

All photographs are by the author unless otherwise noted.

Cover photo courtesy of James Bingham

Printed and bound in Canada by Friesens

Distributed in Canada by Heritage Group Distribution and in the U.S. by Publishers Group West

For information on purchasing bulk quantities of this book, or to obtain media excerpts or invite the author to speak at an event, please visit rmbooks.com and select the "Contact" tab.

RMB | Rocky Mountain Books is dedicated to the environment and committed to reducing the destruction of old-growth forests. Our books are produced with respect for the future and consideration for the past.

We acknowledge the financial support of the Government of Canada through the Canada Book Fund and the Canada Council for the Arts, and of the province of British Columbia through the British Columbia Arts Council and the Book Publishing Tax Credit.

To strong and fearless women and girls, everywhere.

"When the whole world is silent even one voice becomes powerful."

– MALALA YOUSAFZAI,
Pakistani activist and Nobel Prize winner

"Knowing what must be done does away with fear."

– ROSA PARKS,
African-American civil rights activist

"We all look for courage in our own lives. We look for examples of it wherever we can find them because we think if we can learn from other people's courage that will help us have courage in ourselves."

– DEBORAH ELLIS,
Canadian activist and author of *The Breadwinner*

CONTENTS

PREFACE

*"You may not control all the events
that happen to you, but you can
decide not to be reduced by them."*

– MAYA ANGELOU,
American poet, singer, memoirist,
and civil rights activist

The room is quiet and there is just a faint light coming through from the nurses' station outside my room.

I'm not sure what day it is. I'm not sure if I can get out of bed and make it the few feet to the washroom. I'm not even sure if I'll make it through today.

The massive blood clot that has taken up residence in my brain is preventing me from doing so many things.

I cannot see properly, due to the pressure on my optic nerve. I cannot feed myself and my speech is incoherent, so I can't even communicate clearly.

I'm not sure I'll ever be able to do these things again at the level I did before.

The only thing I'm sure of is that Sue is here, sitting nearby, and I know she's watching me even as she keeps an eye on the machine that is monitoring my heart rate, blood pressure, respiration and body temperature, praying that it stays silent, not wanting to hear it loudly beeping, causing a sudden flurry of activity as staff in scrubs use their expertise to stabilize me – again.

I am no longer in an induced coma and, as I lay in my bed at the Health Sciences Centre, in Winnipeg, I have plenty of time to think.

I think about my family. I have a loving wife, three wonderful children and three amazing grandchildren.

I'm not complaining. I've had a good life and no regrets.

I've had adventures, travelling the world from Brisbane to the Black Forest, Cuba to Cairo, Tanzania to Tokyo and beyond.

I have set myself challenges and overcome them, completing 250 marathons in one year, climbing Mt. Kilimanjaro in 21 hours, cycling from Cairo to Cape Town and setting Guinness World Records to raise funds for children in need.

Who is to say I won't overcome this, my greatest challenge yet?

Like my approach to everything, I will take it one (faltering) step at a time and see where it leads me.

That was February 2015. Little did I know that having a clot on the brain would lead me to my greatest adventure yet, The Secret Marathon in Afghanistan.

ONE

FROM DARKNESS TO LIGHT

*"The most difficult thing is the decision to act,
the rest is merely tenacity."*

– AMELIA EARHART,
American aviation pioneer and author

My recovery from the blood clot on my brain, diagnosed in February 2015, was a long and arduous process. It was difficult to get back on track. I knew I was getting there, though, when, with the help of hiking poles, I completed a 5K walk, during the Calgary Marathon weekend in May. By the summer I had begun to think about running again. It was in October that my wife Sue showed me an article from *The Guardian* featuring a brave woman named Zainab Hussaini who had become the first Afghan woman to run a marathon, in the first Marathon of Afghanistan. In the article, Zainab, supported by the non-governmental organization (NGO) Free to Run, talked about the issues she faced during her training. "The children were stoning us, the people said bad words like 'prostitutes, why don't you stay at home? You are destroying Islam.'" She ended up completing her training by running around and around inside her walled garden.

After reading the article, I made a vow. If I could recover in time, I would go to Afghanistan and run the 2016 Marathon of Afghanistan, in support of Zainab's efforts to advocate for women's and girls' freedom and right to run.

◇◇◇◇◇◇◇◇◇◇◇◇◇◇◇◇ FREE TO RUN: MISSION ◇◇◇◇◇◇◇◇◇◇◇◇◇◇◇◇

Free to Run's mission is to use running, physical fitness and outdoor adventure to empower and educate women and girls who have been affected by conflict. The organization supports those living within conflict areas and those who have been forced to flee and live as refugees outside their home countries.

The ability to participate in physical fitness and outdoor adventure activities is part in parcel of important human rights and fundamental freedoms, including the right to health and freedom of movement. Unfortunately, in many areas of the world, there are few opportunities to participate in sports. Women and girls are especially restricted in these areas because of widespread discrimination and traditional beliefs about female roles. In countries like Afghanistan, harmful cultural and gender norms significantly limit the ability of women and girls to engage in activities outside their homes. Particularly in areas affected by conflict, sports opportunities are extremely limited or even nonexistent due to a lack of resources and insecurity.

There is an overwhelming need to develop opportunities for women and girls to become involved in sport and physical education. The benefits of these activities are many. On an individual level, they can help to develop emotional and physical well-being and personal power. At the community, regional or national level, sports programs can be used as a tool to promote gender equity, enhance children's and women's rights, and address harmful discriminatory practices.

◇◇

I took up training with renewed enthusiasm. My sights at this stage were set upon the Calgary Marathon. I would train as I had always done, sticking to my regime of running nine minutes and walking one, fuelling appropriately and doing some cross-training like swimming, stretching and weight training.

My training went well, and at 7 a.m. on May 29, 2016, the gun went off, and Captain Clot-Buster (a.k.a. Martin Parnell) burst from the start line. I wore my homemade superhero outfit, complete with scrubs, a Canada-flag-embossed mask, and goggles. It was a warm day, and all along the route people were shouting out their support. Sometimes they weren't quite sure who I was: "Go Captain America," "You're almost there, Canada Man," and "You're looking good, Captain Blood-Clot," were some of the words of encouragement. But it didn't matter what they shouted out, all the positive feedback helped me to finish in 4:24:40.

I was back.

◇◇◇◇◇◇◇◇◇◇◇◇◇◇ CAPTAIN CLOT-BUSTER ◇◇◇◇◇◇◇◇◇◇◇◇◇◇

On October 24, 2015, I undertook my first serious race since my recovery. Kirsten Fleming, race director of the Calgary Marathon, suggested I enter the 10-km "Dash of Doom." This is an annual event, and runners are expected to wear fancy dress. Kirsten thought I should dress up as a doctor, to show the clot who was boss. I liked the idea, and Sue and I came up with my alter ego, Captain Clot-Buster. Many other superheroes participated in the 10K. I took my place alongside them, lining up in my doctor's scrubs, a Buff with two eyeholes cut in it, and swimming goggles with the lenses removed. The race went well and I came in at 51:21. This time was not only a personal best for Captain Clot-Buster, but Martin Parnell also took second prize in the fancy-dress contest.

◇◇

I am a member of the Canadian Association of Professional Speakers, and at the monthly meeting in mid-March I had met and had a conversation with Kate McKenzie, who, for seven years, had been a junior-high-school teacher but had recently changed careers to become an author, artist and documentary filmmaker. She had read my book, *Marathon Quest,* and was wondering what I had next on the horizon. I told her about the Marathon of Afghanistan. Kate was hooked. As I continued training for the Calgary Marathon, Kate and I kept up our conversation about the Afghanistan event, and plans started to develop to film a documentary of the race. Soon, Kate brought in her cousin, Scott Townend, who is also a documentary filmmaker.

KATE'S JOURNEY: MEETING MARTIN

My journey to Afghanistan began in Calgary, Alberta, while I was trying to decide if I should walk across a room to speak with the Marathon Man – Martin Parnell – a Guinness World Record holder and philanthropist extraordinaire. I had just finished reading his book, Marathon Quest, *which my husband Leor bought for me at an event. Leor had met Martin and immediately caught his infectious enthusiasm. Leor knew the book was just what I needed after taking a big leap in life from being a full-time teacher to being a full-time artist. It wasn't going well.*

I went from having 30 people around me all the time, asking for help and advice, to having entire days where I was sitting alone at home. I had begun to wonder if anything I was doing mattered at all and if I had started too late to be an artist. As I turned the pages of Martin's book, I read about how he started running at 47 years old. Maybe I could still give it a go at 30.

There I was, seeing Martin across the room, and I was nervous to go and say hello. How could I tell him he'd made such a big difference for me? How would I let him know that his book was a lifeline? Everything I thought to say just came off sounding cheesy. What if he brushed me off? I was sure he probably got sick of people talking to him about his book. He probably had more important people to meet. As a former teacher, I have learned that sometimes the words you tell your students come back to haunt you. I remembered that I always taught my students to let people know you appreciate them. You must let people know what a difference they make for you, so I forced myself to walk over, introduce myself and let Martin know the difference he had made for me.

Martin immediately put me at ease with his enthusiasm and self-deprecating humour. We chatted away, and I felt like I had always known him. He mentioned that the next thing he was planning to do required a filmmaker and asked if I knew anyone. I had no idea what he was planning but I felt confident that if Martin was involved it would be an interesting chance to be part of something that mattered. I volunteered to help. I could barely believe that Martin Parnell wanted to get together for a coffee with me!

I first saw Zainab's picture in a Guardian news article Martin sent me. I saw the desert sand dunes under her feet. She looked so determined. One woman against the world. I felt compelled to learn more. I pulled up every article, image and news piece I could find. The article said she was the first Afghan woman to run in the first marathon that had ever been held in Afghanistan. The race organizers enabled women and men to run alongside each other. Zainab used the marathon as a way to take a stand and speak out about the need for equality. She said she wanted to be free to run.

Zainab's story resonated with me. It made me think of all the times I had run searching for freedom. Not freedom from inequality, terrorists or landmines – mental freedom.

Sometimes, I go for a run in the rain because if I cry in the rain it's less obvious. The tears stream down my face and in the shadows of the thunderclouds, my tears and the raindrops blend together. My breathing is laboured as I cry and run, but I feel that if I could just run fast and far enough, my muscles would be exhausted, and my thoughts would slow down. My thoughts spin so fast. Negative thoughts, spiralling me deeper and deeper downward. I think, I'm too tired. I can't do this anymore. Nothing I do matters. Why do I even bother? No one will notice if I don't show up tomorrow. I'm all alone. I think somehow that if my feet can run fast enough, they will catch up with my brain. I reach a moment when I am so physically exhausted that the thoughts finally begin to slow down. I can finally focus on the sound of my feet on the pavement, hear my breath, feel my heart beating, and feel the rhythm of my body. I begin to glimpse a bit of the freedom I am searching for as I run. I can't imagine not being able to run. I must be able to run.

Having dealt with mental health issues for most of my life, I need a release. When I was younger, I closed myself off from everyone and thought I could just handle it all on my own. When things built up too much, I wanted to feel like I could control something, and I resorted to self-harm. I became addicted to the release I would feel. But I was also ashamed of it. I would hide it and make up excuses to not have to wear swimsuits or let anyone know how bad it had become.

I'd like to say I never feel that way anymore. I'd like to say that I'm fine now, that I've recovered, that the mental health issues I faced as a teenager were just products of melancholy, teenage angst, and that now I'm the picture of health, but that would be a lie. It has been 16 years since I've self-harmed, but I still feel that addiction inside me. Now when I feel it, I know I have to do something. I have to find the willpower to put on my shoes, head out the door and go for a run. Sometimes I only walk. Sometimes I only need to go for one block. Other times, I run and run and run, fighting with everything I have until the feeling goes away. There are days when I want to take that part of me that feels things so deeply and just rip it right out.

If I couldn't run, if I couldn't find a release, I don't know what I would do. The idea that Zainab didn't have that kind of freedom really hit me. What if running wasn't an option to find a healthy release? Everyone deserves to be free to run, and I wanted to help.

When we met for coffee, Martin told me that to put on the Marathon of Afghanistan, the race organizers invite ten international athletes to participate. These athletes' race fees allow the organizers to offer the race for free to any Afghan person who wants to participate. Martin planned to go and run. He told me that Zainab's story motivated him to recover from his own illness, and he wanted to run with her and let her know what a difference she had made for him.

"If I bring back some video I shoot on my phone or my GoPro, do you think you would be interested in helping me edit it together?" he asked.

I knew this story was too important not to tell in the best way we possibly could.

"I'm in, Martin," I said. "I want to help. But what if I came with you and shot it?"

I realized I had just signed myself up for what might be the most important story I would ever film. I knew I needed help. I reached out to my cousin, Scott, who is also a filmmaker, to help me co-direct, and I asked Colin and Liam to complete our film crew. I had always wanted to work with Scott on a project. He had so graciously mentored me through so many of my own projects, and I couldn't think of a better person to join me in making this film. We sat down and started talking through the story idea for the film. I told him all about Zainab and all about Martin.

"You've got two larger-than-life characters," Scott observed.

"I know. They're amazing," I said. "Martin ran 250 marathons in one year. Who does that? And Zainab, she had to train in her garden so she wouldn't have rocks thrown at her or face threats from terrorists! I just can't even image it."

"Yeah, but that's hard to relate to," Scott countered. "Where's the average person in this story? Where's that someone that people like me, who don't run, can understand?"

I didn't want people to write off this story as yet another one about larger-than-life heroes accomplishing something epic and out of reach. Those kinds of stories just don't feel real to me. I knew what Scott was saying. Sometimes when I hear those kinds of stories I find myself thinking, I could never do that. We needed to find a way to show that being free – being equal – wasn't just an issue for people in Afghanistan, and it wasn't just a women's issue. We all need to be free.

"You run, right?" Scott asked.

"Yeah, but nothing like a marathon! The longest I ever ran was 10 kilometres, and even that felt like a stretch. What can you possibly think about during more than one hour of running?"

I let the idea sink in. Maybe Scott was onto something. If I ran my first *marathon, we could tell this story knowing the pain, blisters and determination it took to run every single kilometre in training. Before I had a chance to think about it further, I blurted out, "If it helps us tell the story better, I'll do it. I'll run the marathon."*

After the Calgary Marathon, I felt I could proceed with my plan. In early June I met up with Kate and Scott. We discussed the documentary, and for the rest of the afternoon we shot footage for the sizzle reel. The storyline was that I would be training Kate for her first marathon, in Afghanistan!

Scott filmed Kate and me sitting at Kate's kitchen table as I went over the five-month training plan. "What we have here are four running sessions a week, for a total of 80 sessions. That's 800 km and 100 hours of running. This will take you to the start line of the Marathon of Afghanistan," I explained. Kate said nothing and just smiled. She was probably starting to get an idea of what she had gotten herself into.

In mid-July, I headed over to Sudbury, Ontario, to spend some time with our daughter, Kristina, her husband Paul and our grandchildren, Autumn, Nathan and Matthew. During my stay, I told Kristina about my plan to travel to Afghanistan and my reasons for wanting to go. I think this resonated with her and, a few days later, she said she would like me to join her in running a 5-km race. So, on the Sunday before I left, we got up bright and early and headed off to Massey, a small town 100 km southwest of Sudbury. Every year, this town of three thousand, puts on a marathon, a half-marathon and a 10-km race. This year they had added a 5K. We waited at the start line, and at exactly 5:45 a.m. the gun went off. This was Kristina's first 5K, and she set off like a bullet. She then began to slow down but, as we approached the finish line, we both started to sprint and Kris pipped me at the line by 0.1 second.

It was wonderful to have run with my daughter. The 5K gave me the opportunity to chat with her about the different sports we'd done together over the years, including ice-skating, skiing, swimming and tennis. Kris was always quite sporty. She played soccer at the age of five; I was her coach. And in 2006 she even completed a sprint triathlon.

When we returned from Sudbury, my training continued, and in late August Sue and I headed north for the Edmonton Half-Marathon. I was feeling strong. This race was also part of Kate's training program.

KATE'S JOURNEY: TRAINING AND THE HIJAB

I had made the commitment, and now I was scared. Could I really spend that much time alone with my thoughts? Martin generously offered to be my coach. He said he ran without music or podcasts. He felt it allowed him to be more in tune with his body and to make sure he was paying attention and preventing injury. It made sense, but I just didn't know if I could do it.

Everyone always says that the hardest part of a marathon is the mental battle. As someone who was already dealing with mental health issues, how was I possibly going to face added mental pressure? What if I couldn't do it?

I put the training calendar Martin made for me up on my fridge and stared down the 20-week plan he had created for me. "You don't have to do much, you just have to do something," Martin told me. I just had to plug away at it. "Don't worry about the speed. Just get it done."

Eight hundred kilometres of training lay in front of me. It wasn't my first time running, but I had always done much shorter distances. I liked the 400 m in track and field and even managed to enjoy my 5 km on the cross-country running team in college. I got tricked into running a 10-km race once, but really, I just liked short distances. I wasn't looking forward to getting black toes, so I religiously applied Glide to my feet and followed all Martin's other instructions for nutrition and hydration. His strategy for me was to run nine minutes and then take a one-minute walk break to hydrate and take photos and video for our film, and then run another nine minutes. I kept telling myself, "I just have to run for nine more minutes."

Some nine-minute stretches felt like the longest of my whole life. I used tricks to pass the time. I asked Martin if he ever got bored running for so long. "No," he said. "The scene changes every second, just like the frames in a movie." I challenged myself to try and find something interesting or beautiful every second. I sang songs in my head and sometimes out loud while I ran. I listed out everything I was thankful for, and sometimes I resorted to just telling myself, "You can do it, you can do it, just keep going," repeating it like a mantra.

The hardest part of preparing for the marathon wasn't the running at all. It was the unknown. At the end of August, I had run 394 kilometres. I was training for the marathon, but we still didn't know if we would be able to go.

◆

"What are you going to wear?" I think my sister was the first one to ask me this question. I had travelled to other Muslim countries before. In Iran, for example, wearing a headscarf was mandatory, but I had never attempted to wear a headscarf while running. I wanted to make sure I did it in a way that was respectful. Like every other part of my equipment and gear, I would need to test it before going to Afghanistan, and I knew that as soon as I put on a headscarf to do a trial run I would be seen as a Muslim woman running around my city. I didn't want to offend anyone. I didn't want to be disrespectful. I needed some advice.

Martin introduced me to Nada Merhi and the Calgary Muslim Marathoners running club. When I arrived at Nada's house, I saw she had invited some other women from the club to join us. Nada set out an amazing feast for us while we chatted. They shared with me that hijab (meaning "to cover or to veil") is not just about wearing a headscarf, it is about modesty. In order to be respectful while wearing the headscarf, I would also need to draw attention away from the shape of my body by wearing loose-fitting clothes that came to my wrists and ankles. They shared with me why each of them chose to wear or not wear a headscarf and helped me learn how to properly wrap the headscarf so it would not come undone while I was running. As I posed for them with my headscarf properly tied, they congratulated me and said, "You make a good-looking hijabi!"

When the evening ended, Nada handed me a beautifully wrapped box. Inside there were two headscarves with pins and other thoughtful gifts. "These are for you," she said.

I was so humbled. The generosity of the women from the Calgary Muslim Marathoners club was amazing. I was a stranger only hours before coming into Nada's home, and I left as a friend. They had removed one more obstacle in my way and empowered me to do this run. I knew I would wear one of the headscarves they gave me during the race so that, in some small way, their spirit of friendship would be with me while I ran, and I could honour their generosity.

I needed to know how much hotter it was to run with a headscarf. I also needed to make sure that everything stayed in place and there was no chafing. I borrowed a baggy, long-sleeved shirt from my husband, put on a running skirt and long pants and looked at myself in the mirror. With my running belt and running shoes on I looked like I was about to go out for a winter run, but it was late summer and considerably hotter than when I would normally wear these kinds of layers. I stood in front of the mirror as I completed my look. I felt like a different person wearing my hijab. How would people react? Would they be scared of me? Would they insult me? I started to feel scared. Was this how it felt for other women wearing hijab?

As I ran down my block, I suddenly felt that I needed to smile at everyone I saw. I was now a representative of a different culture and a different religion. I didn't want to leave others with a bad impression. People, especially women who passed me, smiled back at me and wished me good morning. In fact, more people smiled at me than usual. Maybe there was hope.

I met Kate at the start line of the half-marathon. Despite the hot weather, she was dressed in a hijab, long sleeves and leggings. She had reasoned that since she would be required to wear this clothing for the Marathon of Afghanistan, she would train and race in it while she was running in Canada. She wanted to see how it would feel to run in what she felt would be rather restrictive gear. A month prior, Kate had spent an afternoon with Nada Merhi and other members of the Calgary Muslim Marathoners. I had coached Nada and the group for a 10-km race and they had offered to help Kate prepare her "race hijab" for the half-marathon. The gun went off and we maintained a 6 minute/km pace and finished in 2 hours, 9 minutes. Sue was at the finish line and cheered us in.

Returning to Calgary, Kate and I had a key meeting regarding funding for the documentary. As Kate says, "Traditionally, when you're making a film you don't keep it a secret. You tell everyone and ramp up the excitement before you've even shot a single scene, so you can find investors and partners to help you finance the film." We couldn't do that. We couldn't even build a website. We didn't talk about the film because we didn't want the wrong people to find out about it and endanger those who were participating in the marathon. Time was running out before the trip, and Kate said we needed to find someone "daring enough to believe that this film might work." I agreed with her. We needed someone who would take the leap and believe that the visas and film permits would be granted and that this story about being free to run was worth sharing.

Kate and I had already been to a few unsuccessful meetings with potential backers when we secured some face-to-face time with the founders of Viiz Communications, formerly a division of Nortel, now a telecommunications provider in its own right. Kate was beginning to think we might not be able to pull it off. But then we met with John Wilson and James MacKenzie, co-founders of Viiz. They were very supportive of the project – John said we had them at "we want to change the world." They agreed to invest $25,000 into the documentary, which would allow a two-person film crew to travel to Afghanistan and film the marathon.

Later, Kate told me that although she had tried to remain calm and businesslike during the meeting, at the end of it "all I could think was *They said yes. They said yes!*" I remember her jumping up and down in excitement after the meeting, saying, "We're going to Afghanistan, Martin!" I was smiling from ear to ear, feeling a mixture of elation, relief and anticipation. John and James had given us the opportunity to bring the story of Zainab and the other Afghan women to a worldwide audience. Our dream was becoming a reality.

After speaking with John and James, Kate and I were in high spirits, but we soon realized that our other partner, Scott, had different feelings about the project. In late August, he emailed me, sharing his reservations about travelling to Afghanistan. He wrote:

My desire to shoot the film and be there for you is at an all-time high, but my desire to actually be in Afghanistan is still at an all-time low. I want to be there for the project, and I want to be a big part of it, but I'll be totally honest, with my reservations about travelling to Afghanistan, I'm not sure I'm the best person for the job. For that reason, my instinct is to tell you that if you know a couple people who have travelled enough to be more comfortable, are good camera operators who might be interested in this crazy adventure ... and you are comfortable with them ... truthfully they will probably do a better job for you because they will be much more comfortable than I would be.

I hadn't known how strongly Scott felt about going to Afghanistan, and his note ushered in a wakeup call for me. I thought, *He's right. Afghanistan is a high-risk location.* I had done my due diligence, but was it enough? I would be travelling with Untamed Borders, a highly reputable company with expertise in travelling in countries where there are areas of conflict, specializing in trips to Afghanistan, Pakistan, India, former Soviet Central Asia and the Caucasus. It also arranges tours to other off-the-beaten-track destinations. My friend and family doctor Bill Hanlon knew James Willcox, one of the company founders, and spoke very highly of him and his company.

Knowing that Bill approved of Untamed Borders was a relief to me, as he is very experienced in travelling to remote and volatile parts of the world with his foundation, Basic Health International, which helps provide access to good nutrition, education and medical care in high-altitude communities in areas such as Ethiopia, Nepal, Pakistan, Peru, Tajikistan and Tibet. He has also spent time in northern Afghanistan with isolated communities at high elevations.

Still thinking about Scott's note, I thought back to the conversations I had had with my friend and fellow runner Chris Shank, a wildlife biologist and project manager for the only national park in Afghanistan, Band-e Amir, about 60 km from where the marathon would take place. Chris had shared his knowledge of travel and conditions in the country. He did tell me one thing he had learned through his regular trips to Afghanistan: nothing is guaranteed. There is always an element of risk there, and things can change, dramatically, at any time, due to the instability of the region.

Sue was especially concerned and reminded me of the many other ways of supporting women and girls. In fact, we had both been doing just that through our years of fundraising for Right To Play. One of its primary goals is to tackle gender inequality. The folks at Right To Play know that, in certain communities, gender inequality is a serious issue. To quote the organization, "Cultural norms and traditions can perpetuate discrimination and stereotypes for women and girls. Barriers to education, the threat of violence, gaps in reproductive health knowledge and social exclusion are among the many challenges facing women and girls."

Right To Play tries to resolve these issues through play-based educational programs, reaching millions of children every year, nearly 50 per cent of whom are girls, and 54 per cent of the organization's coaches are female.

Sue wondered if it was necessary for me to go all the way to Afghanistan, considering the risks the trip entailed, just to run another marathon. Of course, she, too, understood the hardships and inequalities faced by the women and girls there. After all, she was the one who had shown me the article about Zainab. But, having nearly lost me when I was so ill with the blood clot, she didn't want any more worry. The fact that she had lost both of her parents that same year had made 2015–2016 a very trying time. Sue just wanted normality and peace of mind.

Despite all the facts I was considering after Scott's email that might have made someone else change his mind about the venture, I realized I was still determined to support the women and girls racing in Afghanistan. All I could do was assure Sue that I was taking every precaution and was convinced everything would be fine, that I'd come home safe and sound. I'm not sure how reassuring my words were.

With Scott's decision not to go to Afghanistan the hunt was on for a film crew. In early September, Kate secured the services of filmmakers Colin Scheyen and Liam Kearney.

Colin is a documentary filmmaker based in Toronto. His films focus on issues of community, identity and social issues. His documentary feature film *Nuclear Hope* focuses on Canada's nuclear waste issues and has been screened at festivals throughout North America, South America and Asia. It also won the 2015 Rising Star Award at the Canada International Film Festival.

Liam is the director and producer of production and post-production at Liam Kearney Media, where he has worked with clients including Bell, *The Globe and Mail*, Sustainable Design Awards, Toronto Luxury Rentals and the NXT City Awards. He is also the director and producer of the short documentary "This Job Saved My Life" and the series *Convenience Stories*, which, at the time of writing, streams on Bell Fibe TV1.

I was excited to work with Colin and Liam, who were both excited about the project and the prospect of travelling to Afghanistan. Colin said, "I got into documentary film for two reasons: to travel the world and to meet interesting people." When Kate asked him to join our small team, he thought the project seemed like the perfect example of what he intended to do as a filmmaker. When he told his friend Liam that he was going to Afghanistan to shoot a documentary, the two of them were in Colin's backyard enjoying a warm afternoon. A fan of travelling to tourist-free destinations, Liam was pumped right away and thought to himself, *I want to go too!* As Colin told him more about what the project entailed, Liam casually suggested that he'd love to join in, that is, if Colin needed a hand. And so the pair signed on.

Of course, they were concerned about the security risks. Colin maintains that he refused to allow his worries to stop him from going. Later, he told me, "I don't want to believe that there are places in this world that are not worth the risk. That just seems like giving up, doesn't it?" And Liam steadfastly prevented himself from worrying, even when he read the Canadian government's advisory that warned against travel in Afghanistan. "I decided that anxiety about the trip was not a good idea, so I reminded myself that millions of people live there every day, going to work, raising their families. We never hear about those people in the news, so I made sure to remind myself that that was the reality. I also had faith in Kate's planning and Untamed Borders."

Needless to say, both Kate and I were relieved to have them on board. But that didn't mean that our resolve didn't oscillate from time to time.

In late September, I finished reading a book called *The Underground Girls of Kabul*, by Jenny Nordberg. It left me totally overwhelmed. The challenges for girls and women in Afghanistan seem insurmountable. The story highlights several girls who became *bacha posh*, girls temporarily raised and presented as boys. When these girls were asked what being a boy meant, they all said the same thing: "Freedom."

Towards the end of Nordberg's book, I felt somewhat defeated. What good was it for me to go to Afghanistan, what difference could I make? But in her epilogue, Nordberg writes that men "are the key to infiltrating and subverting patriarchy." She denies that the case for women's rights in Afghanistan is a hopeless one. Instead, Nordberg says that hope lies in the men who control what happens to their daughters, that most Afghan men are not fundamentalists. She writes, "In every successful grown woman who has managed to break new ground and do something women usually do not, there is a determined father, who is redefining honor and society by promoting his daughter."

Nordberg's book got me thinking about the trip and my role. I knew I would be listening more than I would be speaking. I also knew that when I did speak, there would be one question I would be repeating: "How can I help?"

TWO

WHEELS UP

"The question isn't who is going to let me;
it's who is going to stop me."

– AYN RAND,
Russian-American novelist and author

On September 20, I received an email from Marvin Pawlivsky of The Co-operators, my insurance company. Things were not looking good for travel to Afghanistan because the Government of Canada advisory for the country had changed from "only essential travel" to "avoid all travel." With a feeling of trepidation, I did some research and found that there were 13 countries under the "avoid all travel" designation: Afghanistan, Burundi, Central African Republic, Chad, Iraq, Libya, Mali, Niger, North Korea, Somalia, South Sudan, Syria and Yemen. It made me realize how fortunate I am, having been born in England and now living in Canada. I have always had access to education, health care, sports, arts and, most important of all, a peaceful existence. Many of the people in these areas of the world have none of that. They exist in a state of ongoing war, oppression, violence and inequality.

Marvin explained that the upgrading of the advisory for travel to Afghanistan was "due to the unstable security situation, ongoing insurgency, terrorist attacks, the risk of kidnapping and a high crime rate." He told me that because of all this, my policy would exclude all sickness or injury, unless I was to get sick or injured doing so-called "normal" activities. Even then, he said, "I imagine there would be a lengthy conversation about whether or not the claim would be valid, given the destination."

I must admit, I was a bit taken aback by this. There were only five weeks to go until my departure, and it felt like my planning for the trip was progressing along the famous pattern of two steps forward and one step back. The situation in Afghanistan was deteriorating, and I didn't even know if it was possible to get into the country. Sue and I talked about the latest developments. In the end, we decided I should contact James at Untamed Borders and get his advice. From the beginning he had said this trip could be called off at any time, and I had to be prepared for that possibility. Now was the time to see if that point had been reached. I knew I would be disappointed if the trip was not a go, but I also knew I had every faith in his decision. With some trepidation, I sent him an email, asking if the trip was still on and if it was where he might suggest a place to get insurance. He assured me that, at that time, it was a go. The only thing I could do was continue with the preparation and training. At that point, he had no advice about insurance.

Over the previous four months, Kate and I had run together only a couple of times. She and her husband Leor had moved to Toronto, and she was doing most of her training in an area of the city called The Beaches. In July, when she was back in Calgary, we headed out to Highwood Pass. This is the highest paved highway in Canada, at 2195 m, and would give us some idea as to what it would be like to run at 2743 m+, Bamyan's elevation. The other time we ran together during that training phase was in early August, when we completed a 20-km run along the pathways in Calgary. Kate told me that she was finding the training hard, but she was sticking to the schedule. I was very impressed with her mental toughness.

My training was going well too, and I had started to put in some long runs on some very familiar territory, the back roads around Cochrane where I had completed some of my marathons during my 250-marathon year.

Kate and Colin had been talking daily in preparation for shooting the documentary. They chatted about the purpose of the film, who they would meet, locations and history. As Colin later said, "With each passing day, [the trip] seemed more and more real."

Even though preparation for the trip and training was taking up a lot of my time, I still had to hold down my job promoting my two books and carrying out speaking engagements. Then the executive director of the Cochrane Public Library, Jeri Maitland, asked me to be its writer-in-residence, a one-year posting. I was thrilled to accept and at 9 a.m. on October 11, I arrived at the library and settled into my office, whose door bore a sign announcing: Writer-in-Residence Is In. I really enjoyed meeting prospective authors and discussing their work and writing processes, from first ideas to publication. My work at the library gave me access to a multitude of books, which was a plus as I continued to read and research for the coming trip.

There was one book I had on my list for trip preparation that I hadn't read by October. Even though it is set in Pakistan, I thought it might help give me some insight into the issues facing women and girls in Afghanistan. That book is *I Am Malala*.

⟡⟡⟡⟡⟡⟡⟡⟡⟡⟡⟡⟡ MALALA YOUSAFZAI: ACTIVIST ⟡⟡⟡⟡⟡⟡⟡⟡⟡⟡⟡⟡
AND NOBEL PRIZE WINNER

When Malala Yousafzai (July 12, 1997) was a just a child, she became a proponent for girls' education in Pakistan, which attracted negative attention. The Taliban issued a warrant for her life, and an extremist gunman attempted to assassinate her on October 9, 2012.

After surviving the bullet wounds intended to kill her, she continued to speak out on the importance of education. Malala said that following the attack, "the terrorists thought that they would change our aims and stop our ambitions, but nothing changed in my life except this: weakness, fear and hopelessness died. Strength, power and courage were born."

Malala also works against illiteracy, poverty and terrorism: "The extremists were, and they are, afraid of books and pens. The power of education frightens them. They are afraid of women.... Let us pick up our books and pens. They are our most powerful weapons."

In 2013 she gave a speech to the United Nations and published her first book, *I Am Malala*. In 2014, at 17 years of age, she became the youngest person to win the Nobel Peace Prize.

◇◇

I raced through Malala's book in two days, all the while thinking about the challenges Zainab deals with every day as a woman in Afghanistan. One of my favourite parts of the book is at the start of Chapter 1: A Daughter is Born, in which Malala speaks about her birth. She was a strong baby from the start and even though she was born in a place where daughters are "hidden away behind a curtain, their role in life simply to prepare food and give birth to children," her father added her name to the family tree, which showed only the male line. Even though the villagers "commiserated" with her mother on the birth of a daughter, and no one congratulated her father, Malala's father treated her with love and respect: "He even asked friends to throw dried fruit, sweets and coins into my cradle, something we usually only do for boys." Even her name suggests the love her parents had for her: "I was named after Malalai of Maiwand, the greatest heroine of Afghanistan." Malalai was a hero who inspired the Pashtuns to defeat the British in 1880, during the Second Anglo-Afghan War. Her father felt she was special, right from the beginning.

That Malala's father championed his daughter reminded me of Jenny Nordberg's book, in which she talked about the "determined fathers" who were one of the keys to change and equality for women and girls in areas like Afghanistan and Pakistan.

Over the years, I've come to realize that people like me, who have been lucky in life, must take a stand and make a difference. Reading Malala's book only strengthened my resolve to venture forward and act in the name of equality. If Malala, who faces so many challenges in her work, can do what she does, I knew I could certainly at least make a contribution. If I could get to Afghanistan at all, that is.

By the time I'd finished reading *I Am Malala*, I was no longer as concerned about my insurance while in Afghanistan (James Willcox had suggested going with First Allied as a broker), but another complication had taken that worry's place. And it was a greater worry: would I even get into the country? My Afghanistan visa had still not arrived, and my departure date was a mere three weeks away. I called the Embassy of Afghanistan in Ottawa and asked for an update. They said they were waiting for clearance from Kabul, which should arrive soon. I waited another week then phoned again – still no luck. This time, the clerk told me to ask Untamed Borders to call the Ministry of Foreign Affairs (MFA) in Kabul, which I did. On October 19, with just one week to go to my departure, I heard from James Willcox:

[T]he man at the consular department ... told me that they have contacted the MFA in Kabul for authorisation to issue you with the visa. He told me that usually they respond much quicker than they have in your case. However, unless they respond with authorisation they cannot issue the visa.... [W]e have never had issues with people from Canada receiving their visas and, as far as I was aware, they have not needed to wait until authorisation from the MFA. Perhaps this is a new policy.

He did suggest that we can contact the MFA on your behalf to obtain an authorisation number for you and they will issue it for you within 24 hours. We have a lot of previous experience with the MFA and this is not a simple or fast process. We will contact them but as the request for permission has been with them since September I am not hopeful that our request will make any difference to the process.

This delay is really something new for people from Canada applying for Afghan visas. We have had people apply in the past, as recently as September this year, and it has been a straightforward process.

Let us hope that they issue the authorisation this week or the beginning of next. We are limited for options for plan B if they do not do so.

Things were getting desperate. That evening I had supper with Chris Shank and Bill Hanlon. Chris shared some stories about his recent visit to Afghanistan, where he had been asked to write a proposal for the continued development of Wakhan National Park, located in the far northeastern corner of the country. This park was established in April 2014 and is 25 per cent larger than Yellowstone National Park in the US. Chris first began wildlife conservation work in the country in the 1970s, and he had returned several times since the Taliban had left the area.

I told them my tale of woe regarding my visa. Bill said he had experienced the same issue when he was organizing a trip to Pakistan. His was an eight-week working trip, and in the end it all had to be cancelled because the visa didn't arrive in time. Chris offered to get in touch with a guy named Arif, one of his contacts in Kabul. He would go into the MFA and find out what was going on.

The next day Chris received an email:

Dear Dr. Chris,
Hope all is well with you there!
Thank you for your email. The experience shows that tourist visa does not need

to be checked with MFA in Kabul. As today is Thursday and the government is off in Kabul. Our admin officer Mr. Farooq can go to the Ministry of Foreign Affairs on Sunday to check and see the circumstance of this issue. Therefore, if possible please send us a copy of the schedule confirmation letter from Untamed Borders. Additionally, we would advise Mr. Parnell to go himself to the Afghan embassy in Ottawa to follow up his visa issue, there is possibility of missing the document/application etc.

Best regards,

Arif

Thrilled with the response, I sent all the required information to Arif and he got back to me first thing on Sunday, October 23, to say I would not need MFA's confirmation for my tourist visa and that it would be best for me "to refer to the Afghan Embassy in Ottawa and explain the situation; they will help you and issue a visa soon. As I mentioned before, there is the possibility that your application could be missing."

That morning I went for a 20-km run. During the two and a half hours I had plenty of time to go over what I was going to say to my contact at the Afghan Embassy in Ottawa.

In the afternoon, I Skyped with Kate. I was very concerned but trying to stay positive. She told me to keep my spirits up. Thankfully, she, Colin and Liam had had no problem getting their visas in Toronto. Kate also had another piece of good news: she and Scott had been working with James Willcox to get the appropriate paperwork to allow filming in Bamyan. It certainly wasn't a guarantee that they would be granted permission, but I was thrilled and relieved to hear that James had told Kate that the appropriate documents had been signed and, once we were ready, filming could go ahead.

On Monday morning, October 24, with only two days to go, I made a call to the clerk at the embassy. I repeated what Arif had said about the MFA not needing to be involved. He told me to phone back in one hour. This I did. He now told me that my visa was ready and would be shipped via UPS. Unbelievable!

I wasn't out of the woods yet. I calculated that the visa had to travel 2882 km in 48 hours (my cut-off time being noon on Wednesday, October 26).

For the next two days I waited, still no visa. On checking I was told it hadn't even been sent out for delivery. I decided to try a different tack. I asked my friend Jason Webb at Downunder Travel for advice, and he suggested I try to have the package delivered right to the airport UPS depot so I could pick it up on the way to the plane. He offered to ask a friend of his at that depot to hold it for me.

The day before I was due to fly, Scott arrived at 2 p.m. to film me preparing to leave and saying my goodbyes to Sue. I only hoped he hadn't had a wasted journey.

I didn't sleep well that night, fretting about the visa. Before going to bed, I tracked the package, and it seemed to be on its way.

Thankfully, by morning, the UPS website told me the package was at the Calgary Airport. Alleluia!

Scott offered to drive me, knowing we'd have the chance to take some film footage of the happy reunion of me with my passport (visa included). When the UPS clerk handed over the package, I worried. It seemed very small. But upon opening it, I saw my passport. I flicked through it, spotted the colourful Afghanistan visa, and let out a huge "Yippee!" In the end, the visa had been delivered to me just six hours before my departure.

Both UPS clerks hugged me, and the manager, Nevin, came out to shake my hand. My relief was palpable, I'm sure.

On the way back to Cochrane, Scott and I came down from our "visa" high. On the way down Big Hill into town, I asked Scott if anyone had come up with a name for the film. He hesitated and then asked, "Has Kate mentioned anything?"

"No."

"Do you have a name for it, Martin?"

"Yes," I said. "*Marathon of Afghanistan.*" Not very creative, I must admit.

He paused and then said, "Look, I'll tell you the name Leor came up with. Say the first thing that comes to your mind after I tell you, OK?"

I agreed.

"*Afghanathon.*"

Now it was my turn to pause. I don't know about you, but the first thing that came to my mind was another cheesy film title: *Sharknado.* I wasn't keen.

It was 1:30 p.m. and I had just one hour to go before heading off to the airport to catch my flight. After all the final packing and last-minute checks, I gave Sue a big hug and told her I loved her and that everything would be fine. Excited as I was to be going on what I viewed as a great adventure, I knew Sue was choking back the tears and would probably worry until I was back safe and sound.

As I was driving to the airport, Scott back at the house interviewed Sue and asked her what she thought of my trip to Afghanistan. She said, "Absolutely it's crazy, some of the stuff he's done, but he's able to use something he really loves to do to benefit other people. So it makes sense. Although this may be one of the crazier things he's thought of doing, I know it won't be the last. I just look forward to the day he walks back through the door."

The next thing I knew I was standing in line at the check-in and the attendant behind the desk asked me where I was going.

"Kabul."

She looked up towards heaven and then asked, "Are you going to join ISIS?"

I was flummoxed and quickly said, "No!" (I'm not sure what she would have done if I had said yes.) "I'm going there to run a marathon."

Then came the fateful words I've heard so many times over the years: "Are you nuts?!"

"I could be," I said. "But this is the second year for the marathon. I'm going over to support women's and girls' running in Afghanistan."

"How did you even know about this race," she asked. I said I was a runner and we had a network of people who shared information. As I walked away, I left her shaking her head.

I would soon board my plane to Frankfurt, a ten-hour flight covering 7500 km. I planned to have supper and watch a movie. *One step at a time*, I thought.

KATE'S JOURNEY: IT SINKS IN

It hit me one month before the marathon that this could be my last month. I didn't know what was going to greet us when we got to Afghanistan. Thankfully, we connected with James from Untamed Borders, who helped us with much of the logistics. However, I had only met him via Skype, and now we were trusting him with our lives. It took us months to find travel insurance that specialized in conflict zones. It was surreal to talk about our insurance for kidnapping, dismemberment, terrorism and death. I prepared my will. I phoned up or messaged each of my close friends to tell them what I appreciated about them. If this was the last they heard from me, I wanted them to know how much I loved them.

It's hard to look into the eyes of the people you love and know that they wish you weren't going somewhere so dangerous. I watched as tears welled up in their eyes. Through forced smiles, they would simply say, "Stay safe," when what they really wanted to say was, "I'm scared. I don't want anything bad to happen to you, and I don't really understand why you need to go and do this."

During the last month leading up to the marathon, with my life and the lives of my crew on the line, priorities became very clear. I wanted to spend more time with my family and friends. At the end of the day, they were what mattered most.

Running became the time I had to go and clear my head. It was the time I had to find calm and peace. As the distances increased, I took solace in the runs as the time when I could take refuge from thinking about the "what ifs" of the film and the race. There was so little time left and so many more things still to plan.

Colin and Liam would be joining me as our crew to help capture the video and audio of the trip. I would also film and direct while I ran. Somehow, amid directing, filming and running I also knew I had to make sure Colin and Liam stayed safe. When we said goodbye to their wives in Toronto, I hugged them and let them know I would do everything I could to keep them safe and bring them back home. I meant it. I knew as the leader of this tiny but mighty film crew, I needed to stand between them and the risks we would face and bear the responsibility if anything should happen to them.

THREE

KABUL

*"If you don't get out of the box you've
been raised in, you won't understand
how much bigger the world is."*

– ANGELINA JOLIE,
American actress and humanitarian

When I was waiting for my visa to arrive, I had made myself a file folder of information about the trip. At 7 p.m. on October 27, I was reclining in the Primeclass VIP Lounge at the Istanbul Ataturk Havalimani International Airport. I had an eight-hour layover and I decided to open the file and have a read.

I first read through the Marathon of Afghanistan package from Untamed Borders. The tips provided would be important, especially the cultural information and the security precautions.

Clothing: *Afghanistan is a conservative country and as such there are social norms we should adhere to with regards to dress. Men should not wear shorts.*

Women should wear a headscarf and long-sleeved, loose-fitting clothes that hide the shape of the body.

Culture*: It goes without saying that Afghanistan is a very conservative Islamic country. Afghan people are generally very hospitable and forgiving if any faux pas are made. The following are some guidelines to ensure that we are good guests:*

- *Always ask before taking photos. Be especially aware of taking photos of women and people praying.*
- *Take off your shoes if entering a mosque or someone's house. Hold the soles together.*
- *Do not walk in front of someone if they are praying.*
- *If you are a male, do not start talking to / interacting with women.*

   Security Precautions*: The areas we are visiting in Afghanistan are areas that we feel comfortable that we can take people without any undue risk. However, things can change, so in order to help maintain a high standard of security please note the following.*

- *Please do not take any photos of any military personnel, vehicles or installations.*
- *We may get invites for tea or for dinner from people. This is one of the great things about visiting Afghanistan. However, we also have to be cautious. Please follow your guide's lead if he feels taking up an invite is inappropriate.*

After reading Untamed Borders' tips, I progressed to the latest travel advisory I'd printed, courtesy of the Government of Canada:

Global Affairs Canada advises against all travel to Afghanistan, due to the unstable security situation, ongoing insurgency, terrorist attacks, the risk of kidnapping and high crime rate. If you choose to travel to Afghanistan despite this

warning, you are taking a serious risk. We strongly recommend that Canadians register with the Registration of Canadians Abroad Service and include personal and professional contact details. If you are already in Afghanistan, you should leave. The Embassy of Canada in Afghanistan's ability to provide consular and other support throughout the country is very limited.

My decision to go had not been an easy one. The advisory was crystal clear: Do not go, and if you're there, get out. But I felt I had to dig deeper. As I relaxed in the comfortable environment of the lounge, I reminded myself that Untamed Borders had extensive experience in the country. By this point, I had had several conversations with James Willcox and had come to respect his experience and ability with risk mitigation. In one conversation he told me, "This is not the first trip to sports events that Untamed Borders has organised in the Bamyan Valley. We have been running trips to Afghanistan since 2006 and ski trips to Afghanistan since 2011. Since 2013 we have been asked by the organisers of the Afghan Ski Challenge to run packages for that event. We came back from running skiing trips to the 2015 Afghan Ski Challenge in March 2016. [And we] do not just arrange skiing in Afghanistan; we have been working for eight years bringing tourists safely to Afghanistan as well as Pakistan, Central Asia, North East India and Russia. We guided 15 groups to Afghanistan in 2015 and have a lot of on the ground experience in ensuring our guests have a memorable time for all the right reasons." I felt I was in good hands for my coming adventure. Certainly his suggestion for insurance had been spot on.

Included in my folder of goodies was my First Allied insurance plan. First Allied specializes in high-risk countries. The package I purchased came in two parts. The first was the standard coverage: personal accident, death and disability, medical expenses and emergency evacuation, baggage theft, damage, and delay. But reading the second part of the policy really hit home: crisis, wrongful detention, kidnapping, political threats, disappearance, hijack, terrorism and violent crime. A sobering list, but at least I had the best coverage I could get for any eventuality.

I believed I was going in as prepared as I could be. Yes, Islamic State militants had only recently kidnapped and shot dozens of residents in a central Afghan community in revenge for authorities having thwarted one of the militants' unsuccessful sheep robberies. Yes, the Islamic State had also recently carried out an attack on a Shia Muslim shrine in Kabul in which 14 people were killed. And just a few months before I was due in the country, suicide bombers had targeted a Shia demonstration and killed 84 people. I reflected that in the *Times* that morning Hugh Tomlinson had reported, "Taliban fighters cut off the highway between Kabul and Kandahar yesterday as the insurgents launched attacks just west of the capital, severing the main link between Afghanistan's two biggest cities."

I closed my folder, determined to stay calm. I felt I had prepared the best I could. I had done my due diligence on Untamed Borders, I had secured insurance that covered as many eventualities as possible and I had done the required training for the marathon. I would arrive in Kabul the next day and only then would I know what was in store. Soon it was time to head over to the departure gate for the final stage of my journey to Kabul. The call went up for general boarding of Turkish Airlines 706, and as I made my way to the check-in, in the crowd, I spotted a guy wearing a "Marathon of Afghanistan" T-shirt. I introduced myself, and he told me his name was James Bingham, the race organizer. There were two women with him, Vicki Burford from England and Irene van As from Holland.

I settled in for a blissfully uneventful flight. As the sun rose that Friday morning, we arrived at Kabul International Airport. Baggage collection and customs went surprisingly smoothly, and by 10 a.m., James, Vicky, Irene and I were walking out into the bright sunshine of a Kabul morning. We walked 500 m and were greeted by three men waving enthusiastically.

One of them was James Willcox, co-founder of Untamed Borders. The other two were guides Kausar Hussain, who is also the other founder of the company, and Gull Hussain Baizada, an Afghan guide.

They welcomed us with warm handshakes and smiles. I felt a sense of relief. I was now in the hands of Untamed Borders, and for the next ten days I would follow their advice and direction in navigating the customs and cultural traditions of Afghanistan.

We jumped into two vans and headed out into the Kabul traffic, which was relatively light. Gull attributed this to it being a Friday and a holiday.

Driving into the city I noticed the wide boulevards with shops lining both sides of the streets. Men, in a variety of clothing, and women, in burqas and hijabs, were going about their daily business, and children were playing in groups of twos and threes. However, the presence of security forces was in evidence everywhere. Several buildings were surrounded by massive concrete walls, complete with barbed wire and gun posts.

After 30 minutes we pulled into a side street and parked next to an eight-foot wall with double gates. The driver got out and knocked on a side door. A man appeared, the double doors were opened and we drove into a courtyard. Entering from the dusty gravel street, as we had, it was like we had discovered another world. The proprietor welcomed us into a garden full of flowers and large trees. Chairs and tables were arranged on the lawn so that we could enjoy an afternoon cup of tea. Walking into the lobby of the Cedar Guest House, I went up to the registration desk and said, "Salam." The clerk replied, "Salam," and gave me my room key. I headed upstairs.

I found the door to the room open, as my roommate, Walter Murray, was already inside and unpacking. We started to get to know each other right away. Walter is from Toronto and works for CBC TV News. "I've done a number of these type of trips," he said. He was not planning on running the marathon but was on holiday and wanted to experience the culture of Afghanistan. I thought I recognized Walter's accent and was excited to hear that he was from Dorset, England, and had played soccer on the reserve team for Southampton Football Club. I told him I was a supporter of Plymouth Argyle FC, and he offered commiserations.

After we had settled in, Walter and I went downstairs to meet the rest of the group. Along with Vicki, Irene and James Bingham were Paula Boast (Ireland), Brad Taylor and Drew Peterson (USA), and Andre Doehring (Germany). All of them would be running the marathon. Brad had run the First Marathon of Afghanistan in 2015, but the rest of us would be running it for the first time.

We were excited to head out and enjoy a day in Kabul, but first James Willcox gave us a briefing that covered security, customs, food and generally what to expect while we were interacting with the local people. He suggested that we might dress in traditional wear, so as not to stand out. I put on baggy pants and a long overshirt, but I wasn't quite convinced that I would blend in. He told us to stick together and to ask him, Kausar or Gull if it was OK to take photos, as some of the locals might object.

With James's advice ringing in our ears, Kausar led us out the door to experience a taste of Kabul. We drove for ten minutes and the first stop was a bread shop. We all crowded into a ten-by-ten-foot room. The whole area was covered with beautiful, colourful Afghan rugs, and to the left of us was a man squatting on a raised platform with piles of loaves around him. Some were round, others diamond-shaped, but the majority were long and thin and as big as skateboards. He would sell the loaves to his customers through a window. In the back, on a lower level, three men, one wearing a dust mask, were preparing the dough, kneading the loaves into the required shapes. They would then lower the loaves into a cylindrical, underground oven. When the bread was ready, they would take it to the front of the shop and stack it there for sale. As we were leaving, a man came up and purchased 30 of the skateboard-shaped loaves. I purchased a loaf and thanked the bakers for showing me around their shop.

As we travelled to our next destination I enjoyed the warmth and taste of the Afghan bread.

Next up was a visit to the Kart-e Sakhi Mosque. Just weeks prior, a terrorist, wearing a police uniform, had entered the mosque and opened fire on a crowd of Shia Muslims marking Ashura, which commemorates the seventh-century death of a grandson of the prophet Muhammad. In total, 18 civilians were killed and 50 wounded. As we walked around, we could see families interacting and being respectful in this very holy place. I was struck by the beauty of the architecture: three large domes surrounded by four majestic minarets. The outside walls were covered with tiling. Each tile was intricately designed with flowers and calligraphy on a blue background. It is said that calligraphy granted Islam a form of art that set it apart from all others.

Leaving the mosque, we walked down some steps, rounded a corner and there, in an open field, was a playground. It had the usual swings, merry-go-rounds and teeter-totters, but unlike the ones I am used to, all the equipment was handmade. The jewel in this gorgeous playground's crown was a hand-cranked, four-child Ferris wheel. An incredible amount of work had gone into the building of this place for children.

This playground was spread out over a large area and the equipment was in relatively good shape, not new, but functional. There was a sprinkling of children using the equipment, and two men were stationed at the Ferris wheel, giving rides. Vicky and Brad asked if they could have a ride, and the men let them. I decided to have a go on the swings and joined a boy, dressed in a shirt and jeans, and a girl in an aqua-blue hijab and purple dress-pants outfit. I think I blended in very well with my baggy brown shirt and pants and Afghan scarf.

It was obvious that this was an important place for the local people. It was located on a rough patch of ground that had been levelled out. I looked around, and on the perimeter were apartments and small houses built into the side of a steep hill. The playground was a little sanctum of peace and recreation. It was somewhere the children could go and be kids, a place where parents could take a break from the daily grind and anxiety of living in Kabul.

The afternoon was spent visiting the garden of Babur – Bagh-e Babur. This place, one of the earliest surviving Mughal gardens, is named for the dynasty's founder, garden fan Zahir-ud-Din Muhammad Babur (1483–1530), who is laid to rest there. It was the perfect lunch spot. We had an incredible view over 15 terraces, across the Kabul River to the snow-capped Hindu Kush beyond. We were lucky to be visiting the garden when we did, as its restoration, back to its historic roots as an Islamic landscape garden, was only completed in 2008. There are layers of spiritual meaning in the garden and its geometric-inspired planting, natural water channels, fountains and cascades that people spend their lives studying. I was told that the garden is a metaphor for divine order and, as a paradise on Earth, a place of refuge for the faithful. As I write this book, the garden is on a tentative list to be a UNESCO World Heritage Site.

We left the wonders of Bagh-e Babur, and Kausar took us to Tapeii-i-Maranjan, a high hill in a southeastern neighbourhood of the city, home to a great many kite flyers. I was excited to see one of the famous kite fights of Kabul! I had read that kite flying was banned during the Taliban regime, from 1996 to 2001, during which time it enforced a strict interpretation of Sharia Law over most of Afghanistan. It didn't surprise me that kite flying had been banned then, but it certainly was popular now, given the number of people we saw on the top of the hill with their kites. Watching this spectacle reminded me of a book I very much enjoyed, *The Kite Runner*, by Khaled Hosseini.

However, not everyone was flying a kite. Amid the clashes of the kites, young men galloped by on horses, and a group farther down the bluff was playing a game of soccer. I should clarify. All the people on the bluff were men or boys. As with many recreational activities in Afghanistan, kite flying is largely prohibited for women and girls.

Kausar told us that since it was Friday, we would be sure to see some action. The men and boys gather on the bluffs to send their kites up into battle. How do kites battle? Well, Afghan kite strings are not simple cotton or nylon but are coated with a concoction of glue and crushed glass, making them incredibly sharp. The goal is to use your kite string to cut another kite down.

While we were there, a van pulled up. I was thrilled to see Kate, Colin and Liam step out. I hadn't seen Kate since she was last in Calgary, and it was the first time I had met Colin and Liam. But there was so much going on that we really didn't have much time to catch up. It was getting late and Kausar had offered to drive Walter, Vicky, Drew, Brad, Irene and me back to the guest house.

◇◇◇◇◇◇◇◇◇◇◇◇◇◇◇◇◇◇ FILMING IN KABUL ◇◇◇◇◇◇◇◇◇◇◇◇◇◇◇◇◇◇

Colin and Liam used Panasonic GH4 cameras when shooting video, time lapses and stills for the documentary, and Liam also used his iPhone 6. Liam told me that the iPhone came in handy sometimes because it was small enough not to draw any attention when he and Colin were advised to be discreet, particularly when driving around Kabul. For audio they used a Zoom H4N sound recorder, a Sennheiser G3-A lavalier mic and a Sennheiser boom mic.

Beginning in Kabul, Kate, Colin and Liam met every evening to discuss the day's events and plan for the following day. Those first few days in Kabul weren't very demanding for their production work, so they "had time to get an idea of the area, get some nice B-roll, and prepare for busier days," Liam said. Colin added that at the end of each day, he spent his evening copying files onto hard drives. Kate directed the content, but Colin, as director of photography, had the freedom to decide the framing for the camera work.

◇◇

On the way back to the Cedars Guest House, I reflected on my first day in Afghanistan. I think the thing that most surprised me was the amount of play I'd witnessed in Kabul. I hadn't expected that. The other thing that surprised me was the energy of the children. Considering where they lived, I had expected them to be sombre, but the ones we had met had big smiles and were enjoying life. One thing I did note, however, was that most of the children I saw were boys.

Sleep didn't come easily with the combination of jet lag and sights of Kabul dancing in my head. At 5 a.m., there was a knock on the door. It was time to leave for the next stage of our adventure. Walter and I quickly got up, packed and headed downstairs. The rest of the group was in the foyer, and one of the guest-house attendants showed me where to find the instant coffee. There was just time for a quick cup before we were on our way in a convoy to Kabul Domestic Airport. The night sky was cloudless, stars showing as pinpricks of light across the black expanse. Next stop, Bamyan Province.

FOUR

THE ORGANIZERS

*"We do not need magic to change the world, we
carry all the power we need inside ourselves
already: we have the power to imagine better"*

– J.K. ROWLING,
British novelist and screenwriter

Two main characters behind the Marathon of Afghanistan are James Willcox (Untamed Borders) – who organizes the trips, bringing people from all over the world – and James Bingham (race director) – who organizes the marathon event. Following are their stories.

JAMES WILLCOX: UNTAMED BORDERS, UK

At 0800 on November 4, 2016, I was not on the start line of the Marathon of Afghanistan.

I've never been on the start line of a marathon.

To date, I still haven't.

I've never run a marathon.

At 0800 on November 4, 2016, I was hurtling down a road in the Hindu Kush, in a van packed to the roof with tables, chairs, water, dried fruit, Iranian chocolate bars, hi-vis vests, checklists, first aid kits and volunteers. Rapidly dispensing instructions and peeking through a crate of bananas, looking out for the cairn of rocks marking 5 km from the start of the race. Hoping that local kids had not dismantled it from when we measured the course the day before.

At 0755 on November 4, 2016, I had been next to the start line of the Marathon of Afghanistan, open mouthed as James Bingham, the race director, told me in all seriousness that the race would be starting on time. I'd been involved in one marathon, six ski races and ten years worth of trips of various types in Afghanistan, and none of them had ever started on time. It seemed that this one would be special, and if I did not get a hurry on, special in a very unfortunate way.

It was almost ten years since I had first been to Bamyan.

That first trip was a major part of why I became involved in Untamed Borders and why I was desperately trying to arrange the checkpoints for a race that was inexplicably going to start on time.

In 2006 it would have been impossible to hurtle down that road in a van. Ten years before the marathon there was no paved road in the entire province of Bamyan. The 180-km journey from Kabul took 12 hours.

I'd first come to Afghanistan on a whim. I'd spent my 20s either bumming around Asia or working in the UK to pay for this bumming. After extended trips to East Asia, Southeast Asia, the Middle East, Russia and the subcontinent, it was only right that Central Asia got a visit. The lost heart of the continent. I instantly fell in love with the region. An area that has so many influences from its neighbours, this was a place where familiar tastes, smells, sounds and sights from previous trips all came together amongst windswept deserts and bare mountains. The centre of Central Asia was Afghanistan, and despite some concerns, I crossed from Pakistan through the Khyber Pass and on to Kabul.

I remember the excitement of bouncing my way to Bamyan in a minibus on the same route that the Silk Road traders would have taken two thousand years before. It was spring and the ride from Kabul was through and up a succession of blossoming valleys. The passengers of the minibus shared salted rhubarb. Slightly unnervingly, most men in the valleys I drove through were armed. It was sowing season and birds looking for some seeds were quickly dispatched, destined for the pot. Afghanistan is a major bird migration route, but given that anyone over the age of 12 is armed I am still amazed any birds survive the journey.

Bamyan was, and still is, a one-street town in a mountainous region in the centre of Afghanistan. It was once famed for having the largest standing Buddha statues in the world. The Buddhas are now rubble, destroyed in a moment of madness in 2001 by the Taliban, but the valley is beautiful, with snow-capped peaks in the distance and a mountainside covered in caves and niches that used to house people, carvings and statues. They give a glimpse of Bamyan's history as a major trading town on the Silk Road during the first to eighth centuries.

At the beginning of the first millennium the Kushan Empire spread in a great arc around the eastern flank of the Himalayas, from present day northern India via Afghanistan to China. It was through the Kushans that Buddhism and Buddhist thinking rounded the Himalayas and reached China and the Far East. Bamyan was the last town on the northern side of the Hindu Kush before the passes that took the traders and pilgrims to the subcontinent. Here the town grew. The cliffs were hollowed out to create places of worship and for traders to build images of the Buddha for luck as they set off into the unknown. The standing Buddhas were some of the last remaining signs of Bamyan's Buddhist history. Even without them, the sight of the mountainside riddled with holes and caves on an epic scale in a place so remote is stunning.

The man next to me on my first drive to Bamyan asked why I was spending a whole day in a bus to see some empty holes. I pointed to the magnificent alpine views outside the window, and he looked at me as though I had two heads. For a boy brought up in East Kent in the UK, Bamyan was a far cry from Dover town centre.

Bamyan is in the Hazarajat, the home of the Hazara people. The Hazaras are descendants of the Mongol hordes that came through here seven hundred years ago. They are also Shia. So not only do they look markedly different to other Afghans, they are heretics in a predominantly Sunni country. This has led to a succession of usually Pashtun-led ethnic cleansing attempts over the years, from the Emirs to the Taliban. Due to the Hazarajat being a maze of valleys deep in the Hindu Kush, none of these attempts were successful and, rather like the Kurds in Iraq, the Hazaras are flourishing under the new regime, allowing children to go school and infrastructure to be built for the first time in their history.

The concept of hidden valleys, lost peoples and Shangri Las in the greater Himalaya range is as old as the mountains themselves. Modernity has mapped this great range, and even the most remote valleys now have contact with the outside world. However, Bamyan retains some of that mystique – not in the classic sense but as a place apart, hidden by mountains, a bubble of peace and calm in a sea of trouble. The fact that a mixed-gender marathon can even be held in Afghanistan is testament to Bamyan's unique character.

On that first visit to Bamyan I met an Afghan translator for the UN called Abdul. He was a nice guy but a little lonely away from his village two days' travel from Bamyan. He was a generous chap, and I stayed in his one-room flat for a couple of nights whilst he tried to get time off work to take me to his village. Ultimately, he couldn't get the time off, but we spent time chatting about the UK, the UN and why he was trying to develop a Texan accent. Also, I helped improve his English. He now knows the word "capsize" (not entirely useful in a landlocked country with no navigable rivers – in fact, when I visited Afghanistan's biggest lake I saw only one boat: it could seat six and was called the Donald Duck) and how to use "pimp" as a noun, a verb, and with "up" as a phrasal verb. In one of his more perverse moments, he mentioned that he thought Adolf Hitler was a courageous man. I ventured that maybe he was actually a mass murderer and that most people in Europe do not hold him in high regard. I also asked him what had led him to this conclusion. His English was good, so I do not believe I misunderstood him. Hitler's courage apparently stemmed from the fact that upon discovering that a game of cricket was to last *for five days, he put all the players to death. It is just these kinds of encounters that are the reason I like to travel.*

On the second day I knew him, Abdul invited me to set up a development organization with him. When I asked him what we would do, he answered, "Education...or human rights...or law...or legal training...or health. It does not matter; we just should set one up." I saw that day how for young people, potential entrepreneurs, the idea of how to make money was to find international donors and work in the aid and development industry. I found this a depressing experience and although I had started to fall in love with the region and wanted to somehow stay involved in the area, a career in development did not seem all that fulfilling. On that first visit to Bamyan I also stayed at the hotel then owned by my mate Sultan. The bottom floor of the hotel is the chaikhana, *which, like most* chaikhanas, *is a restaurant, café, men's club and doss house all in one. In the centre sits a huge, constantly boiling samovar of hot water. A seemingly endless cast of boys and men work there, alternately serving tea, cooking kebabs and rice, or nipping down to the bakery to get more bread using the Afghan store card – a piece of wood in which the bakery carves a notch for every five breads taken. When the wood was full of notches, Sultan would amble down and pay the bakery.*

Sultan and I would chat away the afternoon. He was two years my senior but looked a good 20 years older. He showed me a scar on his left arm that runs from his wrist to his shoulder and talked about his fight against the Taliban in the '90s when he commanded 20 men (this has grown to 70 soldiers over the years I have known him) and about his dead wife and his son whom he doesn't see as he lives in Canada with Sultan's father-in-law. However, he is upbeat and thinks that times now are better than they were.

He asked me to stay in Bamyan on many occasions. He would teach me Dari, I would teach him English and help fleece the very small stream of tourists that at that time came to town.

It was tempting, very tempting – certainly more so than a life creating Abdul's development organization. His mention of living in Bamyan and "fleecing tourists" was something I had already been considering. I had recently made friends with two Pashtun men. One, Alum Jan from Peshawar in Pakistan, and the other, Hussain, from Jalalabad in Afghanistan. They had discussed how I could help them develop tourism in the region. Alum Jan and Hussain worked with international people, predominantly professionals such as journalists, researchers and photographers. But sometimes with tourists. Their dream, they said, was to one day only guide tourists, as no journalists or researchers would come. "Tourists not terrorists" was their motto. I hung out with Alum Jan in Peshawar for a few weeks and loved the way he and Hussain showed people Pashtun culture, the history of this far-north, western edge of the Indian subcontinent where the mountains meet the plains – the way they enjoyed the adventure of showing international people around the region, despite the obvious risks they faced and because they clearly loved this region that I was gradually falling in love with too. We spent a few weeks drinking tea, eating way too much pilau and chatting politics together. Discussing how we would change the world one punter at a time.

After spending time with them I agreed to help them set up a website to try and promote their trips. I never really saw it as something I'd be too heavily involved with even though they suggested I join them in a partnership. After a week in Bamyan I started to feel that perhaps there was a real opportunity to start a business. That Alum Jan and Hussein were right. Bamyan was a place apart. Somewhere special, untouched, where we could show people an Afghanistan that is traditional and historic and has a stunning landscape.

I was interested, not, like Abdul had suggested, in starting an NGO to "fix" Afghanistan but to show how it can be a desirable place full of great experiences. I understood then and even more now some of Afghanistan's problems. However, these are not the only narratives of the country. My thoughts and feelings for the country come predominantly from another narrative.

So, the three of us decided we would try and encourage people to come to Afghanistan, not because it is broken but because it is beautiful.

Within a year I was back in Bamyan with our first tourists as Untamed

Borders. This was my first time as a tour guide in Afghanistan. I've been leading groups to Bamyan a few times a year for a decade now.

Getting to Bamyan from Kabul has always been an adventure. We bounced along unpaved or snow-covered roads in those early years. Once flights started, things did improve, but it is still an adventure. The first commercial flights landed on an unpaved strip where sheep had to be cleared before the planes landed. One winter we memorably had to give one of the planes a push when it got stuck in the mud. With a paved landing strip, things slowly improved but even then, there are always potential causes majeures: weather, mechanical issues, and on one occasion a mob storming the runway to stop a plane landing after a politician had been refused boarding for arriving too late in Kabul. It's been an eventful ten years in terms of us getting people to Bamyan, back in one piece, and on time.

Using the mountains of Bamyan as a backdrop for sports was an idea that first came up in 2010.

The marathon could never have happened though without an event called the Afghan Ski Challenge. The brainchild of Christoph Zeurcher, a Swiss journalist who was stuck in Bamyan in 2010. As a Swiss he saw mountains, snow, and had free time so his thoughts turned to skiing. Finding out that there were no skis in Bamyan, he vowed to return the following winter with skis and set up a ski race. No one there could ski, but Christoph's pure bloody-mindedness made the event happen, and now the race is a central fixture of the calendar in Bamyan. It is so successful that other organizations have also created ski races in the province. Bizarrely, one was sponsored by the Afghan Intelligence Agency.

My connection with skiing in Afghanistan began in 2009 when I bumped into a Scottish lad who worked for an Afghan development agency. Ken was hiking with his girlfriend in the Wakhan region in the far northeast, the only other region safe enough to consider these types of outdoor trips in Afghanistan. He told me of a group of British and French skiers working in Afghanistan who regularly skied near Kabul in the winter, and if I was serious about being an

Afghan tour operator then I should be offering ski trips to Afghanistan. I said I'd join him on a trip that winter.

On the first trip I made we took one of our regular drivers, Ali. For someone who has never seen skis it is quite hard to explain what we planned to do. Once we loaded up the sticks and skis he had a rough idea of what we were up to and wanted to help. At the bottom of the Salang Pass, which crosses the spine of the Hindu Kush, Ali stopped at a small teahouse and ordered food for all of us. As any Afghan will tell you the best thing for breakfast if you are going to spend all day in the snow is cow's foot. Boiled for hours, this gelatinous lump is exactly as appealing as it sounds. We made a quick note that for the commercial trips, we wouldn't let the drivers choose the dining options.

It was then that I saw how skiing was something that really appealed to all the Afghans who saw it. I stood next to Ali and we watched Ken fly down the slopes. He was awestruck. "He is a djinn," was Ali's response. Hazaras believe there are mountain spirits, and clearly Ken was one. In the teahouse where we stopped on the way back, Ali regaled the owners with the tale of Ken's exploits. Ken was described as a djinn and I as a boz (goat). Keeping with Afghan tradition, the story was heavily exaggerated, but it started a long discussion about skiing, mountains, snow conditions, avalanches and Afghanistan's future. Ali was not the only one who became a convert. I realized that, cow's foot aside, this was an awesome way to experience Afghanistan in the winter. Skiing was very foreign, but the snow and the mountains provided a common factor. I thought Bamyan could be the perfect place for skiing, with its mountains and better security (compared to other places in Afghanistan).

At the same time an international development agency, the Aga Khan Foundation (AKF), saw the potential of promoting tourism in Bamyan as a way of giving the people of the province an additional source of income. The foundation has helped develop guesthouses, organize cultural festivals and provide information about the places of interest in and around Bamyan. That's fine in the summer when tourists come to the valley, but what about in the winter, when *guesthouses lie empty? Well, the people of Bamyan fall back on their timeless winter pastime of just surviving.*

It was clear that any winter income was better than none, so the AKF took a cue from other mountainous developing countries and began a skiing program in Bamyan. With no infrastructure or lifts, the idea was to make the Koh-e-Baba Mountains a new destination for ski-touring.

In 2010 two American skiers were employed for the winter to map out potential routes. They brought only their own equipment, so the Afghans had to get creative if they wanted to ski along with them. Anyone with a small knowledge of Afghan military history will tell you that not having state-of-the-art equipment has never stopped the Afghans. For a people who have battled against the greatest superpowers of their age – the British, the Russians and the Americans – skiing with no ski equipment was nothing. Strips of wood with battered oil tins for edges were constructed.

It quickly became clear that the mountains of Bamyan were perfect for skiing, so in 2011 the AKF hired a foreign ski trainer, Italian Fernando Rollando, who arrived to train the first batch of Afghan ski guides. It was also early in 2011 that a young shepherd, Ali Shah, met Fernando at his village of Khushkak. Ali Shah was fit, young and spoke good English. Fernando asked him what he wanted to be.

"An engineer," said Ali Shah.

"Why you wanna be an engineer? In Kabul there are a thousand engineers. You shoulda be a mountain guide. It's the best job in the world. You spend your whole life in the mountains with beautiful women."

It may not have been a textbook interview, but Ali Shah is now Afghanistan's best ski guide, and Fernando's singular teaching style formed the basis for the success of the AKF's skiing project.

In 2011 the annual Afghan Ski Challenge race (Rule number one: no weapons) was organized by Christoph Zeurcher and has become a focal point for the ski season. With most Afghan challengers having only one month's ski training, the Swiss organizers thought it an unfair challenge. They divided the race into

Afghan and non-Afghan categories. The challenge is a classic ski-touring route that includes skinning up as well as skiing down. They were right to divide the competition, as most of the Afghans had finished before the foreigners even got to the top.

At the time of writing, the event is approaching its ninth year, and the Bamyan Ski Club gets support from St. Moritz (the Swiss resort) and the ski brand Völkl. There is a separate ladies event. Two Afghan skiers, Sajjad Husaini and Alishah Farhang, trained to compete at the 2018 Winter Olympics.

Untamed Borders has been bringing skiers to the event every year since 2012.

As noted, Christoph's efforts laid the foundations for the Marathon of Afghanistan, because the ski challenge proves that a sporting event can be run in Bamyan and have a positive effect both for people visiting and for the people living there.

Bamyan has always had great potential for mountain and sports activities, and in the spring of 2016 it was no surprise that Gull Hussain Baizada, a driving force behind the Afghan Ski Challenge, asked me what I thought about holding a marathon in Bamyan. I thought it was a great idea, and, after giving him a "1 per cent inspiration, 99 per cent perspiration" talk, I suggested to him that the main drawback was that I knew way more about organizing marathons than he did and what I knew could fit on the back of a cigarette packet. However, I knew someone who might be able to help him.

That person was James Bingham.

I knew Bingham from some of his climbing and running adventures in Afghanistan, as well as an ultra race he directed on the Isle of Anglesey. He knew about arranging running races, had been to Afghanistan, and was clearly not quite right in the head. I doubt there was anyone alive more qualified. As it happened, Bingham was looking for a new challenge, so I put him and Gull in touch. At the time, I thought if a race were held, Bingham and Gull would arrange it and my company would run packages for people wishing to compete. Gull and Bingham had a couple of Skype chats, but things were moving slowly, so I said I would meet up with Bingham and see what we could do as a threesome.

Bingham and I met in May 2016 in a pub on Commercial Road in London, then we had a curry. There were three of us in total: Bingham in a business suit (he'd come over from Canary Wharf where he works as a banker of some description), me, and Zyggy. Zyggy is a mutual friend of Bingham and me. I met him many years before, in Peshawar in Pakistan. He once borrowed Bingham's suit, which he then wore to climb Mount Everest. Zyggy is a gentle guy, but with his shaven head and stocky build he looks handy.

With Russian topographical maps of Afghanistan on the table, we thrashed out what we would do. We talked about routes, financing, contingency plans, security risk, the Taliban, ISIS, checkpoints and all manner of tangential travel chat. Pints of Guinness and Tyskie came and went. During pauses in the conversation, I could feel neighbouring tables stop eavesdropping and return to their own conversations. We must have made an odd group: a stocky Pole with shaved head (the muscle) and a sharp-suited Brit (the finance) being shown various maps and security info by yours truly. By the time we went for the curry, an old man by the door stopped us and said, "I don't know what you're planning, but good luck, lads."

A plate of lamb chops and a kilo of pakoras later, we'd thrashed out a plan.

Shortly after the meeting on Commercial Road, Bingham mentioned an organization called Free to Run, a development organization that plans outdoor activities, including running for women in Afghanistan. The founder was Canadian ultra-runner Stephanie Case, who was also a human rights lawyer for the UN. At the time, she was based in Gaza. He was dead set on getting Free to Run involved and having women enter the race. I was sceptical. I'd worked in Afghanistan for ten years and as a foreign man I'd learned that anything to do with Afghan women was likely to end in trouble. I'd pretty much avoided all Afghan women for ten years and was reluctant to start engaging with them.

Bingham was still keen and thankfully ignored my concerns. As a result, Free to Run has been instrumental in enabling the race to have as many female entrants as it has.

Within four months of that curry, we'd got seven international runners and

150 Afghan runners (half of them female) on the start line of the marathon and 10-km course. We'd managed to put on Afghanistan's only mixed-gender sporting event, and we saw the first Afghan woman complete a marathon in her own country. That first year we had a simple plan: put on a race, try not to spend too much money, and take lots of nice pictures. Once we had done it once, we knew we would be able to make it sustainable through sponsorship.

It was not all plain sailing, though. The 2015 race came just weeks after a major assault by the Taliban in another part of the country. It had captured (albeit briefly) the provincial capital of Kunduz – Afghanistan's sixth-largest city. The atmosphere in the country was tense in the weeks that followed, and we constantly reviewed security reports. On arrival at our hotel in Bamyan just before the race, we asked if we could put up the flags for the race in the courtyard, both for a bit of publicity and to check they were all working. As we did so, the hotel staff started laughing. Our flags were white, the same colour as the flags of the Taliban. The staff joked that we were the advance attack.

We considered the 2015 event to be a success. We'd lost some money but had some decent media coverage, both locally and internationally, and we had proved that an event could be done. The hard work was now to start. We needed to make it financially sustainable. I was adamant that the way forward was to get sponsorship from Afghan companies. This is not the usual way of thinking in Afghanistan. Usually events look to government or to donor money from development organizations. However, Afghans use mobile phones, airlines, and banks and drink energy drinks just like the rest of the world. These companies have advertising budgets. To make the funding, and hence the race, sustainable in the long term, we had to tap into local companies. It also appealed to my narrative of Afghanistan: Afghanistan is an inherently valuable place, and by extension so is the Marathon of Afghanistan. Why would you not pay to be associated with Afghanistan? It's amazing.

In the spring of 2016 I finally sat down and shook hands with representatives of Etisalat, one of Afghanistan's major telecommunication companies. As far as sports sponsorship deals go, it is probably one of the smallest ever seen, but along with the entry fees of the international runners, Etisalat's contribution covers the cost of the race. After that meeting I went for lunch alone. For most people the finish line is the high, the pinnacle of the race, but for me that tea and kebabs in Kabul on an overcast spring morning was one of the happiest moments of this journey. My runner's high.

For me, the objective is simple: to arrange an event that stands by itself, funded by people who want to enter the race or want to be associated with it. I know Afghanistan has lots of problems. Some could lead the country into full civil war soon. But when I think of Afghanistan, or talk about Afghanistan, or visit Afghanistan, I think of the things I love about it, like I do with any other country. And I see the marathon in the same way.

Fast forward to 0800 on November 4, 2016. There were 250 runners, including runners from six provinces of Afghanistan and 11 different countries, including a female runner from Iran. Half the runners were women. There were both Shia and Sunni Muslims, from all major ethnic groups. In a country often divided on gender, ethnic or religious lines, the coming together of so many different people was a powerful statement. In addition, there was me in the speeding van, finally finding the cairn we had left the day before.

We unloaded the table, banners, flags, food and drinks for my checkpoint and sent the rest of the crew on its way. As they sped around the corner, the first marathon runner was approaching, police escort and press vehicles in his wake.

I gave my team a quick briefing on how we'd take down numbers and times and feed and water the runners, and then we were set.

Runners I knew came past. Running 26 miles is pretty impressive by itself, but we also had some pretty amazing runners competing that year. I gave a running commentary on some of them to my team. An American guy based in Kabul who is not only a jogger but also juggles, making him a "joggler." In fact, we discovered, he once held the world record for the fastest marathon ever joggled. Past us came Charlie from the UK, an amputee with one leg. In a country that has been so affected by landmines, he was a real inspiration. We saw a bunch of runners from Kabul. On social media I'd seen one of them post that he would win the race. When I had seen them at the start line I asked which one of them had posted that he would win. They laughed. "We all did."

Slowly the time between runners grew, shepherd boys herded sheep down the road. Some men from the NDS, Afghanistan's intelligence agency, came to chat. "Who is winning?" "Is it really 26 miles?" "Can we take some selfies?" Some of the Afghan press took photos, and boys from the villages came to say hello. We handed out Afghan flags for the boys to wave, and we all tucked into spare watermelon and dried fruit that we would not need for the runners.

Towards the back of the field we saw Martin Parnell, another world-record holder after once running 250 marathons in a calendar year. I sensed my team starting to think I am a teller of tall tales. But inspiration did not only come from the runners. For a while, it looked like my team would not have any English speakers. I speak minimal Dari, barely better than the day I first came to Bamyan, chatting to the other passengers in the minivan. However, I knew I'd be able to get the team to hand out water and take down numbers. Still, I was happy when Amina showed up.

She should have been in Kabul at the time of the race, studying at the American University. However, earlier that year gunmen had stormed the campus, killing many students, including friends of hers. Classes had been shut for the rest of the semester, so she had returned to her home town of Bamyan. When she heard about the race, she was in contact with us and volunteered to help at the marathon.

We chatted for a long time about Afghanistan. As it turned out I had seen much more of her country than she had, and I told her about Mazar-e-Sharif and the stunning shrine of Hazrat Ali. Everyone wants to go in the spring to see the flowers of Mazar-e-Sharif, and she said she was jealous. We took a few selfies and photos of the runners, chatted the day away and left as friends.

My race had started a long time before the start line and November 4 was simply the final few metres.

Since the race I've been making plans for future marathons in Afghanistan. Local sponsorship continues, and with Etisalat's help the event should become a regular fixture in Afghanistan. We are working on creating a mixed-gender marathon-training group to give more local runners the training needed to be able to compete.

Every year we hope to grow the race, make it more inclusive, make it better, so that the runners and the community benefit as much as possible from it.

Not that the race is any kind of solution to the problems facing Afghanistan or the future of people like Amina, kept from her studies for six months by an attack on her place of study. In the same way, tourism is also not any kind of solution to Afghanistan's myriad problems and neither is a foot race. However, Afghanistan does not only have to been seen through a prism that only focuses on problems.

I am not remotely qualified to solve any of the major problems facing Afghanistan. But I can be part of arranging a fun event, so I will continue to do so.

My company has continued to arrange trips across Russia, the Middle East, Central Asia and East Africa. This has included arranging a wedding on the edge of an active volcano in Democratic Republic of Congo and the first ski descent of Iraq's highest peak, Mt. Halgurd.

The success of the Marathon in Afghanistan has led me to work on another marathon, this time in Somalia, and to be part of a team developing a ski-touring race in Iraq.

I see the development of sporting events in unusual places as something that is true to what I and Untamed Borders try to deliver. Trips and events that are beneficial both to the people who visit and the people of the places visited. That has always been our ethos, and we hope to continue that in our own small way around the world.

Some of the runners from the 2016 Marathon of Afghanistan want to come back and run it again. Not that they had a great time despite the risk, despite the hardship, despite the dodgy flight, but they had a great time in Afghanistan, period. This is what makes it.

JAMES BINGHAM: RACE DIRECTOR, UK

"Get back, get back, back, back, back!" I shouted as we desperately struggled to keep control. We were on the verge of being totally overrun. Four of us pushed heavily against the office door with all our might. It was me and my brother Ollie, plus a policeman and a local photographer. On the other side stood myriad local Afghans eagerly pushing their way forward. In this chaotic scene we were somehow registering local runners for the Marathon of Afghanistan. The small dust-quilted office formed part of a compound that served as a tourist information centre. Positioned beneath the giant Buddha niches carved into the steep sandstone cliffs towering behind, it was a dramatic location and would be the starting point for the marathon the following morning.

Within the fray, small children, perhaps no older than six or seven, had come to register for a marathon and were now being squeezed and crushed by the enthusiastic mob. We'd momentarily open the door, just enough to pull one or two little ones in, carefully trying to release the pressure without the crowd overrunning us. There was only one door into the office, and once someone registered the only means of leaving was to clamber out the window. This remarkable scene continued like this for several hours.

Later that evening we returned to our nearby hotel with just a few hours remaining to complete the final preparations ahead of race day. It had been a wild, exciting, fun and somewhat emotionally charged day. Most important, we had registered hundreds of local Afghan runners for the marathon and associated 10-km race. Tomorrow would be the third edition of the Marathon of Afghanistan and it was set to be the biggest race in the country's history, with hundreds of runners signed up and many women and girls running.

I'm James Bingham: 42 years old, married, father of two young children. I work for an international bank in London. I am also the co-founder and race director of the Marathon of Afghanistan.

I grew up in a small seaside village on Anglesey, an island off the coast of North Wales. It was a lovely place to spend my childhood – we made our own adventures playing on the beach, clambering around the rock pools. Later we discovered the mountains of Snowdonia, which were right on our doorstep. My dad was into hillwalking, and we climbed Tryfan together when I was seven. As a young lad from North Wales I had no lofty aspirations, but my expeditions have taken me all around the world, from the summit of Mt. Everest to the highest mountains of Afghanistan and Alaska.

After university I moved to London and started running to get fit before heading off on mountaineering trips. I liked the simplicity of running, the fact that I could go for a run anywhere and anytime, with minimal kit compared to the mountaineering. It was easy to squeeze into my schedule, which had become busy with work and two young kids. I could even run to the nursery with a double buggy, and that's exactly what I did for a while.

Afghanistan…? Well it all started in 2009 when I was commuting to work and received a text message from my good school friend Quentin. "Fancy climbing in the Hindu Kush?" I had no knowledge of the area and assumed these remote mountains in Afghanistan and Pakistan were off-limits given the security situation. *The Hindu Kush?* That's Afghanistan, *I thought. Isn't Bin Laden on the run somewhere in those mountain Badlands?* Well, it wasn't quite as straightforward as that, and perhaps it never is in Afghanistan. I found that Afghanistan is a patchwork of communities and provinces, and there are areas removed from the troubles that plague much of the country. We also discovered that a small number of intrepid adventurers and tourists had continued to visit the area over the years.

Quentin's text was certainly a catalyst, and in late summer 2010, two friends and I found ourselves perched on the summit of Mt. Noshaq, Afghanistan's highest peak. We'd become the first British team to summit the mountain since the Soviet invasion more than 30 years earlier. We travelled overland through Tajikistan, over unsurfaced roads, which allowed us to sneak into Afghanistan via a small and remote border crossing in the far northeast. Here on the border zone between Pakistan, Tajikistan and China, the jagged snow-capped mountains of the Hindu Kush unveiled themselves in a striking display of natural beauty. The journey we took, travelling independently with old school friends, the generosity and warmth of the Afghan people, the stark beauty of the landscape – it was an incredible trip that changed all of us. I think we all fell in love with Afghanistan.

In the winter of 2011 I returned on another climbing expedition, this time to attempt the north face of Mir Samir, a mountain in the Panjshir Valley featured in Eric Newby's classic tale A Short Walk in the Hindu Kush. Unfortunately, no success this time – poor snow conditions and the theft of a kit bag scuppered our success, but it remained another incredible adventure.

I was hooked and returned with another friend in the summer of 2013 to attempt an unsupported run of the Wakhan Corridor. This panhandle of land, flanked by mountains on either side, is one of the most beautiful places I'd ever seen. Its inhabitants are nomads who live in yurts and are more concerned with the welfare of their animals than anything else. I'd traversed the base of the corridor in 2010 and was tantalized by what I'd seen. It was around 320 km to the border with China, and we planned an out-and-back run that would span ten days. My running buddy Phil joined me, and we carried everything we needed on our backs. We camped without a tent to save weight, drank water from the rivers and often ran long into the night to make up distances. Running through the Wakhan Corridor was an incredible experience and one that started to make me think about the possibility of arranging an adventure race in Afghanistan.

Back at home I'd set up an ultramarathon called the Ring O' Fire, which involved a three-day, 217-km circumnavigation of the Isle of Anglesey, where I spent my childhood. I set the race up with Quentin – he's a good guy to talk to if you have a wild idea and need a bit of encouragement. The race became well established over the years and importantly allowed me to gain race-management experience. It was really this combination of planning expeditions to Afghanistan, coupled with setting the Ring O' Fire up, which gave me the confidence to ultimately arrange the Marathon of Afghanistan.

Ever since I had run through the Wakhan Corridor I dreamt of setting up a race in Afghanistan, but the years went by and I started to doubt if it would ever happen. Then out of the blue in April 2015 I received an email asking me to help set up a marathon in Bamyan Province. The email was from a man called Gull Hussain Baizada, whom I'd never met or spoken to before. Gull is a local Afghan entrepreneur and travel guide. He was involved in the Afghan Ski Challenge and played a big part in that event's success. Gull had great contacts in Bamyan and this was vital, as we needed the support of the local community. Gull knew about our adventure race the Ring O' Fire and also my love of Afghanistan, and that I was interested in organizing a race.

Both Gull and I also knew James Willcox, the owner of Untamed Borders, an awesome adventure travel company that specializes in arranging trips to remote countries like Afghanistan, Pakistan and Somalia. Their experience of arranging trips to Afghanistan helped to put the travel packages together, and charging internationals to come and run would help finance the event and, most important, meant local participants could run for free.

The fourth annual Marathon of Afghanistan took place in October 2018. The original race was the first mixed-gender sporting event in the country. I thank all our partners, supporters, sponsors and volunteers. I am proud to have played a part in bringing this event to life and to witness the smiles and enthusiasm of the locals who proudly participate each year.

FIVE

BAMYAN VALLEY

In the Afghan people, I found the most resilient,
welcoming people who, for the first time
in my career, never judged me over my right
to tell this story – as a woman or a foreigner.
A people who cherish their culture and history
and the films that have captured that culture.

– PIETRA BRETTKELLY,
New Zealand filmmaker

The flight to Bamyan left at 7:45 a.m., and there was a palpable sense of anticipation within the group. The mood was quiet and nobody said much. At the domestic terminal we had to go through four pat-downs and a luggage X-ray before we were admitted into the waiting area. The 30-minute flight included coffee and breakfast, which really hit the spot. One thing that did catch my attention was a slogan, "Kam Air – Trustable Wings."

As we came in for the landing, I could see small dwellings in Bamyan Valley flanked by the mountains of the Hindu Kush. The landing was smooth and two vans were waiting to pick us up. After a short drive, we stopped at a lookout point – the landscape around us was awe-inspiring. We faced a massive cliff and you could see two excavations in the cliffside. Kausar told us that the cliff once held two legendary statues of Gautama Buddha, one 35 and the other 53 metres tall.

◇◇◇◇◇◇◇◇◇◇◇◇◇◇◇ THE BUDDHAS OF BAMYAN ◇◇◇◇◇◇◇◇◇◇◇◇◇◇◇

The Big Buddhas were carved out of the sandstone cliffs between the third and sixth centuries, when Bamyan was a thriving Buddhist centre. In the early part of the seventh century BCE, Chinese Buddhist monk and pilgrim Xuanzang was perhaps one of the first people to record impressions of the massive, plastered, jewel-studded statues. In his *The Great Tang Records of the Western Regions*, Xuanzang records his journey along the Silk Road, including his impressions of the largest of the two great statues: "Its golden hues sparkle on every side, and its precious ornaments dazzle the eyes by their brightness."

Sadly, the statues did not remain as dazzling as they were when Xuanzang visited them in around 629. As Fabrizio Foschini, of the Afghanistan Analysts Network, wrote in 2013, "It is not clear who damaged the statues before 2001. According to many sources it took three bigoted invading armies to wipe them out completely: Aurangzeb, the sixth Mughal emperor, tackled the legs in mid-18th century, while amir Abdul Rahman defaced them in 1893 (although in some of the first European sketches, drawn in the early 19th century long before Abdul Rahman was born, the statues already look faceless)."

In 2001 the Taliban's spiritual leader, Mullah Mohammed Omar, ordered the total destruction of the statues, as he considered them idolatrous. Taliban soldiers used rockets, anti-aircraft missiles and tank shells, and then they forced some of the native inhabitants of Bamyan, the Hazara people, to help them destroy the statues. Some of these people were hung from ropes and told to drill into the tops of the niches to set explosives. Then, stacks of ammunition, land mines and sticks of dynamite were placed at the foot of the statues. When everything was ready, cameras recorded the devastation of the Buddhas, which had stood for so long, larger by far than any of the other "colossus" statues of the ancient world.

◇◇

Beyond the absent Buddhas, I spotted an incredible number of caves scattered all over the face of the cliff, once used as dwellings where second- to fifth-century Buddhist monks lived and practiced their religion long before the existence of Buddhist monasteries. These caves served as *caityas*, or shrines, for the monks, whose community there, right on the Silk Road (halfway between Rome and China), granted Bamyan its golden age.

We got back into the vans and continued towards the outskirts of town. Soon, I noticed a field dotted with the ruins of burnt-out Russian tanks, artifacts from the Soviet–Afghan War, a Cold War event that started in 1979 and went on for ten years, with the mujahideen (backed by the US and others) fighting against the Soviet Army and Soviet occupation.

Signs of past conflict were all around us. However, it was not just the sight of the tanks that was strange but also the presence of a farmer in the field, ploughing, going around those tanks as if they were trees or large rocks, just another part of the landscape.

Arriving in Bamyan, we approached a bridge and, beyond, a street full of shops. And then we came to our lodgings, the Gholghola Hotel, named for Shahr-e Gholghola (variously translated as the City of Sighs or City of Screams). This was the citadel in the middle of Bamyan Valley that was conquered by the Mongol Empire in 1222. It's said that either Genghis Khan's grandson or nephew died in this battle, which prompted the order for all in the citadel to be killed once the fort was taken. I learned that it was only a 20-minute walk from the hotel to this site of former horrors. In the meantime, in the hotel driveway, a guard combed our van for bombs, even looking underneath with the help of a mirror.

Even though Bamyan Valley has an incredible history of conflict, it was still relatively peaceful when I was there, compared with the rest of the country. It is only recently that the overland trip between Kabul and

Bamyan had been made fairly safe, and by December 2012 the domestic airlines were able to offer flights to the Bamyan airport. Previously, you could only fly to Bamyan if you'd registered with the UN or a recognized NGO. I'd read and heard that Bamyan was where Afghans went on holiday, and I could see why. The valley was beautiful, living up to its name. Bamyan, after all, means "place of shining light," and indeed the clarity of the air here at this high elevation was incredible.

The Gholghola Hotel would not be out of place at an airport or in any of North America's resort locations. Its expansive marbled lobby is two storeys high and dominated by four of the largest chandeliers I have ever seen. The hotel was built by a construction mogul, Hajji Nabi Khalili, who is also the brother of a former vice-president of Afghanistan, Karim Khalili.

When Walter and I picked up our room keys we were told that the sauna opened at 5:30 p.m. and we were free to use the hotel fitness centre at any time. James Willcox suggested the group grab some breakfast, and we all trooped into the dining room. There was porridge, granola and pastries, but I decided to go for their variation of a full English breakfast: boiled egg, sausages, tomatoes and baked beans.

At 10:30 Kausar herded us out on a walk to the Bamyan Bazaar, which turned out to be the street of shops I had spotted on the way in. This market stretches 500 m and includes hundreds of stores. The variety of items available was mind blowing: books, cloth, clothes, fruit, jewellery, kitchen needs, school supplies, stationery, water jugs and so on. I noticed a few "speciality" side streets, catering to specific tastes; I gave them all (fairly) obvious names.

Meat Street had butchers on both sides. On the ground outside one shop I saw the head and hooves of a goat. Kausar said these were cooked and eaten as a soup for breakfast, a dish called *kaleh pacheh*.

Tin Pot Alley had rows and rows of aluminum pots, pans and teapots, along with other utensils such as knives, forks, spoons and cooking stoves.

Nearby was Blacksmith Avenue, consisting of several blacksmith shops, each with its own small forge. The forges were all roaring and the smithies were making horseshoes, nails, picks and shades.

Kerosene and Tire Boulevard. Now there was definitely a safety issue on this street. Shops were full to the brim with kerosene tubs and tires. Kausar mentioned that it was on this street that cars and motorbikes could be repaired. I have since read that what I saw in that market was an insight into Bamyan's history when the place was a busy cultural and trading centre on the Silk Road. I found an article from January 2015, in which *Financial Times* journalist William Dalrymple wrote about the evidence of the intense variety of items that must have changed hands in Bamyan during its golden age (the third to sixth centuries CE). It was a time when cultures met and exchanged goods and ideas. "Archaeologists have found painted glass from Antioch, inlaid gold vessels from Ctesiphon, porphyry from Upper Egypt and lapis from Badakhshan, as well as ivories from Kerala, carpets from Persia, and lacquers, paper and silk from Xian and the great cities of Eastern China. It was through this now remote valley that rival ideas of dress and decorum, philosophy and religion, painting and court culture passed backwards and forwards."

I ambled around, taking in the sights and smells and sounds of the market, and then I made my way back to the main street, where I spotted two boys selling corn-on-the-cob. They had a wheelbarrow containing what looked like a wok. In it was a pile of hot cinders, and in the cinders were several ears of corn. Kate looked on as Liam and Colin filmed my interaction with the boys. I asked one them, "How much for a corn cob?" He put up two fingers. I handed over two afghanis and said, "Salam." He then dug one out of the hot cinders and gave it to me. It was a bit crunchy but very tasty.

This was a highlight of the day, interacting with the local people in the market. This could happen anywhere in the world between a tourist and a vendor, but the fact that it was happening to me in Afghanistan made it very special. Finishing my snack, I ambled back to the shops where I bought a scarf and three journals.

While I was walking around the bazaar, Kate, Liam and Colin were filming the hustle and bustle of the market. If the first morning in Bamyan was any indication the footage was going to be amazing. Later, Liam told me about a young man he met in the market that day. "I had only about 30 minutes to wander through the market. Westerners don't exactly go unnoticed there, and within two minutes a friendly young man approached me and explained that he was studying English at the university there. He was so excited and curious about my presence there and ended up accompanying me and translating for me as I walked through and bought various wares to bring home."

At lunchtime, Kausar took us to a *chaikhana* – a tea room. There were no tables or chairs, just a huge carpeted room with a strip of plastic running down the middle, in place of a table. We all sat crossed-legged as the food was brought out. First, bowls of fatty lamb stew, then pork shish kebabs, rice and salad. To finish we had Afghan tea, a ritual we would be treated to wherever we went in Bamyan.

While we ate, I had the chance to get to know Kausar a bit better. Born in Peshawar, Kausar has travelled every inch of Pakistan and Afghanistan and has friends almost everywhere, from the bustling bazaars of Kabul to sleepy, poppy-growing villages in the tribal areas. When not leading tours and helping to run Untamed Borders, Kausar works as a photographer and journalist. For ten years he has worked with foreign correspondents, affording them access to restricted areas in Afghanistan and Pakistan. Kausar speaks nine languages and for the last five years he had spent time teaching English to Afghan refugees based in the camps that surround Peshawar. I was impressed with his work.

Meals were always good times to get to know the people who had travelled to Bamyan, like me, for the marathon. During supper I chatted with one of the other international runners, Drew Peterson. Drew was from the US and was running his first marathon, although he had previously run three ultramarathons. He works for Goldman Sachs in New York. However, prior to that he completed two tours of duty in Afghanistan with the US Air Force.

After dinner I met Taylor Smith, who works for Free to Run in Afghanistan. She invited me to participate in the organization's events over the week leading up to the marathon. These included a training session for the women and girls who would participate in the 10K and marathon, and a hike. I was thrilled, thinking this would give me a chance to get to know the people of the area and the marathon participants better.

◇◇◇ STEPHANIE CASE – FOUNDER OF FREE TO RUN ◇◇◇

Stephanie Case is a human rights lawyer and women's rights advocate with expertise in conflict settings and humanitarian emergencies. Since 2009 she has worked for the UN in Afghanistan, the International Rescue Committee in South Sudan, the Organization for Security and Cooperation in Europe in Kyrgyzstan, and the UN Office of the High Commissioner for Human Rights (OHCHR) in Palestine and then in Geneva.

Stephanie has witnessed first-hand the harmful effects of conflict and its negative impact on women and girls. She founded Free to Run to use the power of sport to transform lives and communities in the places where it is needed most.

An avid ultra-runner, Stephanie has won or placed in several international running events, ranging from 250-km multi-day desert races to 322-km non-stop mountain races.

◇◇◇

Taylor worried that there might be an attack during the marathon. "Having the start and finish at the same spot and in town might be a problem," she mused. She also worried about the plan to announce the race on the radio that coming Thursday. But even as she worried, she pressed on, continuing to organize Free to Run's Autumn Sports Week events. She asked Kate, Colin, Liam and me to spend time at the local girls' school. I offered to lead a running workshop sometime during the sports week, and Taylor was delighted with the idea.

◇◇◇◇◇◇◇◇◇◇◇ FREE TO RUN: AFGHANISTAN ◇◇◇◇◇◇◇◇◇◇◇

Afghanistan is one of the most challenging places in the world to be a woman. It frequently ranks amongst the lowest of countries in terms of educational opportunities, life expectancy, health and access to justice. Despite significant advances that have been made since the fall of the Taliban in 2001, human rights organizations have reported a regression in women's rights at this writing.

Free to Run supports women and girls in Afghanistan and provides them with opportunities for empowerment and education. The organization launched its programs in Afghanistan in September 2014, thanks to financial support from RacingThePlanet and friends in the running community. The first Free to Run office was established in the Central Highlands region in January 2015. Free to Run operates in three Afghan provinces, providing regular sports activities for students at the high-school and university levels, including hiking, running and skiing. Free to Run also provides international sports opportunities, including comprehensive team training for those who possess leadership potential.

◇◇

The next morning, Kate, Colin, Liam and I headed out with Taylor to the airport to meet some of the female marathon runners who were coming in from Kabul – Fatima, Behishta,[1] Zakia, Zahra, Nelofa and Nazala are all from Mazar; Hassina and Atefa are from Kabul; Habiba is from Bamyan; Raihana Raha is from Diakondi; and Mahsa is from Tehran, Iran. We headed to the Noorband Qala Hotel to set them up with their lodgings. Connie Schneider from Free to Run was also there and held an

---

[1] *Behishta is not her real name. I changed her name in the book to protect her identity. Zahra is also a false name.*

orientation session for everyone. I had been introduced to Connie just the previous week via email, and it was great to meet her in person.

After everyone was settled in, I spent some time chatting with Atefa. She told me that running in the streets was tough and she always tried to find a quiet area where there were no cars. She said one day she was running and two men started to run next to her. She thought they might be trying to chase her but then realized they wanted a race. She increased her speed and got to her home before them. As they continued along, they shouted, "You're a very fast runner."

It was time for the trip to the girls' school, but it turned out that men were not allowed into the school. I went along for the ride anyway, and when Kate and the other female runners went in, Liam, Colin and I went with Kausar on a bit of a walkabout.

The school was on the side of a hill, and we hiked up the road towards the mountains. Kausar said that in the winter people travel this road for about one hour into the mountains to ski tour.

◇◇◇◇◇◇◇◇◇◇◇◇◇◇◇◇◇◇◇◇ BAMYAN SKI CLUB ◇◇◇◇◇◇◇◇◇◇◇◇◇◇◇◇◇◇◇◇

The Bamyan Ski Club was founded in 2011 and is an active club that helps the local economy. Since its inception, the club has focused on its members and their desire to engage in adventure. As a non-profit volunteer organization run by its members for its members, the club strives to organize events that are thrilling, including the annual Afghan Ski Challenge.

The Afghan Ski Challenge is a backcountry ski race that happens every spring in Bamyan Province. The event is open to everyone. Competitors come from countries all around the world, including Australia, Finland, France, New Zealand, Norway, Slovenia, the UK and USA.

Over the years, dozens of local Afghan boys – and, since 2013, girls – have learned to ski (and about avalanche safety) with the Bamyan Ski Club ski school, which operates every February before the Afghan Ski Challenge.

◇◇◇

As we walked, Kausar pointed out several new homes that were under construction. One was a four-storey mansion, almost complete. "Probably belongs to a warlord," Kausar commented. He said it as if this were just a normal occupation, a way for people to get ahead in Afghanistan. I didn't say anything but thought that the challenges facing this country are many and will take a long time to overcome.

Several children walked past us and Kausar asked one boy how far he walked to school. "Seven kilometres there and seven back," he replied.

After picking up Kate and having lunch, Kausar told us we would be meeting up with James Willcox and the rest of the Untamed Borders group, then heading out to see Shahr-e Zohak, the Red City. Now in ruins, the strategically placed sixth-century city once guarded the entrance to Bamyan Valley, high on the hills above where the Bamyan and Kalu Rivers meet. It is situated at the eastern limits of the Bamyan plateau where the road splits, one way leading to Shibar (at the western end of Bamyan Province) and the other to Hajigak Pass (at the northern end of Maidan Wardak Province, connecting to Bamyan). The towers are especially interesting, made of mud brick on stone foundations, wrapping around the side of the cliff. The city was named for a Zohak, an evil character in *The Shahnameh*, a Persian epic poem by Ferdowsi. I'm told that the dynasty that ruled Afghanistan from the 11th to the 12th centuries CE, the Ghurids, also claimed descent from Zohak, who forcibly took control of Iran and was seduced by the devil, who left him with a snake-like appearance and a hankering for human brains.

We slowly made our way up a steep trail to the massive fort. I had spotted several white-painted rocks just off the trail and asked James Willcox what they marked. He said they showed where land mines had been. Dogs were used to sniff out these improvised explosive devices (IEDs), and when found, red-painted rocks would be set down to show the mines' locations. Then a demolition crew would come along, deactivate the mines and spray the rocks white. "Stick to the path," he suggested, "just in case."

This was the first full day of filming in Bamyan and area for Kate, Colin and Liam. They were getting into their stride, with Kate directing the shots, Colin as lead camera person and Liam as lead sound person. The trip to the Red City had enabled the shooting of some incredible footage showing the history and landscape of the area.

The trail wound its way past the fort, up to a ridge and an amazing view of the surrounding countryside. As the sun set, James took part of the group down. Kate, Colin, Liam, Drew and I stayed, as Kate wanted to interview Drew about his experiences, being deployed to Afghanistan by the US military.

Drew explained that both he and his brother, Noel, had joined the US forces and had gone into different conflict zones. He had spent two tours in Afghanistan and experienced some terrible things. One was a trick the Taliban would use to stop military vehicles. They would send a child to run out in front of an armoured truck. If the vehicle stopped, it would be blown up; if it didn't, the child would be crushed. Another was meeting a woman serving a prison sentence of lifetime solitary confinement for having been the victim of rape, which is considered a crime.

"It was very depressing," said Drew. "Women have no rights here....For Afghan women and girls, doing any physical fitness or following their passions is really frowned upon. Fitness and running are viewed as statements that women can pursue anything they want."

Drew joined Goldman Sachs through the Veterans Integration Program (VIP) in 2014. He learned about the program from a friend. "I was done living in a tent," he said. "I felt like I had checked this box in my life and wanted to move on." So, while sitting on a tarmac underneath a tent in 2013, he completed his application to VIP, was accepted and started in April 2014.

In adjusting to civilian life, Drew said one of his biggest challenges was to find that sense of purpose that he and others feel so strongly while in the military. "I have a strong personal connection to Afghanistan," he said. "The people are amazing and are incredibly thankful for American support. People tend to get so caught up in the macro and political discussions in the region, but the average person in Afghanistan just wants to have a decent life, to raise a family and be safe."

Drew started his own charitable organization called Mortales, which is focused on partnering with companies to provide goods and services to war-torn countries. The organization's first mission was for Drew to go with his brother, in November 2016, to the Ukraine, visit two refugee camps at the front lines and provide food and shelter to them.

That day, up on the ramparts of the Red City, Drew told Kate that he was in Afghanistan to give himself some closure. He said Afghanistan "gets in your blood."

After Kate wrapped up the interview, we walked down the trail looking at the magnificent yellow and red silhouette of the fortress. By the time we reached the bazaar, it was dark and most of the shops were closed. It had been a great day, but I was happy to get back to the hotel.

At supper that night, I was hoping to continue my conversation with Zach, which I had started to have at breakfast that morning. For the last ten years, Zach had worked for an NGO compiling a yearly survey on the people of Afghanistan. It is called the "Afghanistan Survey" and is available online.

A summary on the home page states for the 2017 survey:

In a nation undergoing complex change and transition, Afghans continue to weather challenges: a fragmented political system, a decline in aid and growth, and ongoing security and terrorism threats. Even in the face of often seemingly imperceptible progress, Afghans are eager for a better future, and recent data reflects this sentiment. In 2017, the number of Afghans who say the country is moving in the right direction has increased. The downward trajectory

in national mood which began in 2013 has reversed, and optimism has risen slightly this year. However, security fears and economic concerns color Afghan attitudes about the future of their country. More Afghans indicate they would be willing to leave the country if afforded the opportunity, the second-highest level recorded to date. Almost all Afghans believe corruption is a problem in all areas of their lives, consistent with last year's data.

Before his work on the survey, Zach had helped set up circuses across Afghanistan. Zach was a juggler. I asked him if he had heard about "joggling," running and juggling at the same time. He told me that, in fact, he had held the Guinness World Record for the fastest marathon joggling, but the record is now held by his nemesis, Michal Kapral. "I know Michal," I said. "He once interviewed me for a running magazine."

Unfortunately, Zach wasn't at supper. The conversation at the dinner table covered the coming marathon, the runners and who was the current favourite. Also, Kausar told us some amazing stories about medical practitioners in Afghanistan. One that sticks in my head is the man Kausar called "The Bonesetter."

"No need for X-rays, doctors, splints or pain killers, The Bonesetter would realign the bones, and that was it," he said.

SIX

SCHOOL IN A CAVE

"One child, one teacher, one book, one
pen can change the world."

– MALALA YOUSAFZAI,
activist

With dreams of broken bones still dancing in my head, I woke at 5:30 a.m. and decided to go for a run. It felt great to put on my running gear. It was another crystal-clear morning. I switched on my Garmin and waited. It took a couple of minutes for the watch to switch from the satellites over Cochrane, Canada, travel thousands of kilometres, and find the satellites over Bamyan, Afghanistan. I walked through the security gate, said "Salam" to the two guards, turned left and headed out of town. The first 1 km almost killed me. The altitude really took its toll. It felt like I had a vise on my lungs. Slowly, I began to feel better, and I took some photos as I went along. There were a few cars and bikes, and I greeted everyone I met with "Salam."

At the 1.5-km mark I passed an older gentleman. The next thing I knew, I could hear the pounding of footsteps approaching me from behind. The man was keeping up with me. Not only keeping up but pushing me to go faster. We ran together for about 500 m and communicated in sign language. I told him my name but couldn't get his, so I have since thought of him as "Mr. Afghan." After a while, he stopped, and we shook hands. I gave him a hug, and he lifted me off the ground, twice. We waved goodbye, and I carried on my way. At the 2.5-km mark I turned around and headed back to the hotel. Everyone I passed either waved or said "Salam."

The rest of the day was a tour of Band-e Amir park, Afghanistan's first national park, established in 2009. It comprises a series of six deep-blue lakes separated by natural dams made of travertine, a mineral deposit. The park is in the mountains of the Hindu Kush at about 3000 m elevation, west of where the Big Buddhas once stood. I had heard some people liken Band-e Amir to the US's Grand Canyon and that it drew thousands of tourists every year.

The first part of our journey to the park followed the marathon route. I noted the steady uphill climb, thinking *This run is going to be a killer*. After about 60 km, we turned off the paved road and proceeded onto a gravel one. As we crested a hill we saw the aqua blue lakes of Band-e Amir. We dropped down to the car park and spent the afternoon walking around one of the most naturally beautiful areas I have ever experienced.

A section of the walk took us down a single-track pathway cut into the side of a cliff overlooking one of the lakes. I met a conservation officer who said he knew Chris Shank and spoke very highly of him.

As we approached the tourist information centre, I spotted something that made me do a double take: 12 swan-shaped paddle boats tied up along the lakeshore. This was an opportunity that couldn't be missed. I climbed into one of them with Walter, while Drew and Brad grabbed a second and Vicky and Irene a third. We enjoyed cruising around the lake. It was a beautiful sunny day. We spotted birds amid the reeds, searching for food.

A waterfall, multicoloured due to the minerals it contained, created a dazzling curtain against the cliffside.

We could have been at a resort anywhere in the world, enjoying a day out. In fact, several Afghan families were doing just that. In one four-seater boat was a mum and dad and a boy and girl. They were all laughing as the girl splashed water into the boat.

It would be hard to beat a day at Band-e Amir, but when Tuesday dawned, I knew it would hold its own particular riches, as I would be running with the Free to Run girls and women, as well as with girls from a local school. Then some of us were going to visit the caves I had seen on my first day in Bamyan. It only took us 20 minutes to get to the field where the Free to Run girls were waiting. They were already part way through a stretching routine. We joined the circle, and Mahsa had us bending our bodies into many different shapes. It was then time to run. I explained to one girl that I did run/walks, and she seemed to like that idea. We completed four loops around the playground before Kate, Taylor and I headed off with seven of the girls to drop them off at their school.

One of the girls was a real chatterbox: she had lots of questions! She wanted to know where I lived, what the weather was like, whether or not I was married, and if I had children. She also wanted to know if it was easy to move to Canada. I answered as best I could. When we arrived at the school, the girls wanted to show me the volleyball court. It certainly needed some work. Even though the posts were bent, the net was in tatters and rocks and broken concrete littered the playing surface, they were very proud of it.

After about 30 minutes the girls went back into the school, and Kate, Colin, Liam and I met up with Kausar, who drove us to the caves. On the way, he told us the caves, originally created and used by Buddhist monks, housed internally displaced people from a fighting zone north of Bamyan. In the first cave we visited we met Marzia, a mother with five children. Two of the children were at school, but the three others were with her in the cave. One of these was a six-year-old girl named Freshta, who was lying on the floor of the cave, seemingly oblivious to our presence. The mother told the story of how her daughter had come too close to an exploding IED and had been traumatized.

Many of the displaced people who moved into these caves did so to escape poverty and war in other provinces. Moving to the caves was a way to ensure shelter, obtain work in the potato farms nearby and find a way to start over.

Marzia said life was difficult in the caves, and it certainly looked hard. According to an Associate Press article in November 2016 about the Bamyan caves, about 242 families make a life in them. But I also read that authorities were working to relocate the families living there in an effort to protect the archaeological significance of the caves, some of which have ancient murals, perhaps the oldest oil paintings on Earth. UNESCO has called the "cultural landscape and archaeological remains of the Bamyan Valley" a world heritage site that represents both Buddhist and Islamic religions, as well as 1st- to 13th-century art. Even as people made a living in the fields and lived in the caves, Bamyan Province was working to restore the caves, as well as that fearsome fortress, Shahr-e Gholghola. The idea was to have everyone moved out by 2018 to try to save the art remaining in the caves, and Marzia was waiting to hear from the government about when her family might be given an apartment and a new life elsewhere. As of this writing, all Bamyan cave dwellers have not moved from the caves.

The cave Marzia lived in was 3 × 3 m, with a stove in the corner and pillows for sleeping around the perimeter. Her husband was away working, so Marzia was responsible for everything. During our visit, she offered us tea. She had so little, yet she treated us as guests and was so hospitable. As we were leaving, Marzia brought Freshta outside to say goodbye. The little girl started to scream, she was so afraid.

We said goodbye and walked away. We were silent, trying to process what we'd just experienced. In a while, Kate asked me what I thought, and I told her I felt completely overwhelmed having seen the struggle that Marzia and her children had to face every day.

Filming in Bamyan was different than filming in Kabul. Colin said it was not as challenging, except when it came to negotiating the terrain, which, in the end, he said, "only added to its beauty." Both Colin and Liam agreed, however, that it was sometimes difficult to film certain parts of our time in Bamyan, "particularly when we met people who had suffered incredible hardship and trauma," Liam told me. "The hardest time to shoot was after we visited Marzia and her family in the cave," Colin said. "It was so hard to focus on anything after that." Liam added, "There were times where I felt that what I was doing was voyeuristic, and I had to come to terms with the fact that I was there to accomplish a specific task, and that involved documenting my surroundings and the people within those surroundings."

◇◇

My spirits were lifted when we arrived at a school situated in one of the caves, not far from Marzia's home. At the entrance were 20 pairs of small shoes. As I entered, 20 pairs of eyes looked up at me. The teacher said "Hello" and I took a seat in the far corner. The school was amazing. On one wall was a whiteboard for the teacher. On the other walls were examples of the boys' and girls' work, the alphabet, the weekly schedule, children's drawings and much more. Each child came up, said his or her name and read from the board. I taught them to say "Bravo" and clap after each presentation. The children's ages ranged from four to 11.

The hour we spent in the school was magical, and the young female teacher, who was only 18, did a terrific job engaging the children and encouraging them to learn, in a very difficult situation.

On our way back to the van, we saw a group of young boys using a catapult. I joined in and we had a blast shooting small rocks at a boulder. Soon that game was over but just as I was walking away I spotted a soccer ball. I picked it up and began to juggle. The boys pointed across the road and ran off. I followed them and entered a grove of trees. Suddenly there was an opening and, to my surprise, a dirt soccer field. Game on!

I spent 20 minutes kicking a ball around with these children. This game confirmed what I have always believed: that sport is a great equalizer and overcomes any barriers of language, culture and religion.

I spent the afternoon walking up and down the bazaar. I needed a break during this day of mixed emotions. Then I went back to the hotel, had supper and went to bed.

On Wednesday morning I went for a run with Kate. We wanted to do a full test of our race-day gear, so we kitted ourselves out with fuel belts, mics and GoPros. Colin and Liam were all set to film us, using the van as a mobile filming unit. They went ahead as Kate and I hit the streets.

During our first walk break, I decided to give Kate a pre-race pep talk. I told her that she had completed four run sessions a week for over 20 weeks, yielding almost 800 km in training and that this was like a deposit in a bank. Now it was time for the payout, and that was the marathon. I continued that she should run her own race. Kate had been torn between running with the Afghan women or running to her potential. I told her that the Afghan women would not be thinking about running with Kate.

The route we picked ran uphill for 2.5 km and then returned downhill, just like the marathon course. During our second walk break I talked to Kate about what happens next. I told her that the day after my Marathon Quest 250 was over, someone asked me, "What are you going to do next?" I didn't have an answer. However, two months later Sue booked me into the Comrades Marathon in South Africa. She knew I'd need something to focus on, after a very intense year, rather than being left in a kind of limbo. She was right. It's important to have something to keep you motivated. It led me to continue setting myself challenges and raising money for Right To Play, in different ways.

"So, after this marathon," I said, "I have my Seventh Annual Run/Walk on December 31. After that I'm running a 150-km ultra in celebration of Canada's 150th birthday." I also revealed to Kate that I really wanted one of the Free to Run women to come over to Calgary and run that race with me.

I told Kate this story to help set her wheels in motion – what would come next for Kate? She told me that her goal was to, one day, qualify for the Boston Marathon. For a marathon runner, that's a great goal to have.

We finished our run in just over 33 minutes, and Colin and Liam said they were very happy about how what they'd started calling the "Filmmobile" had performed. Colin said he had filmed from the sunroof and out the back door.

By afternoon, we were ready for a hike with the women and girls from Free to Run. We drove on a bumpy road to a small village and piled out. Taylor paired everyone up for the hike. I would be with Kubra. When we chatted earlier in the week, Connie had told me she wanted me to hike with Kubra because she wanted me to talk to her. As part of a three-person (two women, one man) team, Kubra had attempted to run a 250-km, six-day ultra in Sri Lanka, but she had been forced to drop out after the first day. Since then she hadn't trained much but she still wanted to run the Marathon of Afghanistan.

"I feel she should run the 10K instead, Martin," Connie said. "Maybe you can convince her to do this."

As Kubra and I started walking up the mountain trail, we engaged in conversation. Her English was excellent. She told me about her early years, her family and the issues they have had to face. She also spoke about her running and how she had been trained and supported by Free to Run. Kubra explained that she had been inspired by another Free to Run team that competed in an ultra – Nelofar and Zainab's all-woman team.

Kubra told me she had been a student at the University of Kabul until a few months ago when a bomb killed several of her fellow students. Only a few minutes before the bomb went off, she had been talking to a male friend who died in the explosion. This episode had left her shaken and distraught. She left school and tried distance learning, but it didn't work for her. She said, "I will try school again in the new semester," but until then she was working.

As we were chatting, Colin and Liam caught us up and asked if they could record us. So we stopped and I did a mini-interview with Kubra. This is how it went:

Martin: So, Kubra, when I run, I take a water bottle and I might have my running watch and maybe a chocolate bar. But you ran with some different gear. Is that correct?

Kubra: Yes, we had water bottles [and] a bag, and at first everything seemed fine, but we suffered verbal and physical abuse. You know, in Afghanistan, when two alone girls are running on the street during the day, for security protection they need something else with them. So I and Arzoo, my teammate, we decided to have some security equipment. I had a knuckle duster and Arzoo used to carry pepper spray.

Martin: A knuckle duster? Like the metal ones you see in the movies?

Kubra: Yes, yes. I had it in my hand in order to protect myself if anything happens, right?

Martin: OK, so why did you feel the need to have protection?

Kubra: We used to run in the early morning when it was dark. There weren't that many people about, and we were afraid that somebody would attack us or injure us so we decided to have these things with us in order to protect ourselves.

Kubra was excited about the marathon, which was by then only two days away. However, after my chat with Connie, I felt obliged to broach the subject that she do the 10K instead. I said to her, "At the moment are you injured?"

She replied, "No, I'm not injured."

"So, have you trained?"

"I didn't train much."

"I'm going to make a suggestion: I think you should do the 10K and enjoy it."

"OK," she said, reluctantly.

"For the amount of training you've done, I think it would be a good idea. It's your choice, and it's not an easy choice is it?"

"No."

"It's very difficult and it hurts the heart because you want to do it," I continued.

"I want to do it," she replied.

Despite being very disappointed, she did understand the reasoning behind this suggestion. But I saw the look on her face – it was obvious she really wanted to run the marathon.

Kubra and I were still chatting and hiking when Connie called out that it was time for lunch. Unbelievably, we had already climbed for a couple of hours. The view back down across the valley was incredible. The area holds a stark beauty, with rock outcrops and a desert-like landscape. Very little rain falls in this location, and the shrubs are small and hardy. The air is crystal clear but thin; we were above 3048 m at this point. I felt we needed to take a break and recover.

After lunch, 13 of us took part in a team-building game led by Connie. The group was a mix of overseas runners and Free to Run women. The exercise required us all to be blindfolded. We were to hold on to one long piece of rope and somehow form a square. One of the bilingual Afghan women communicated with the group. First, we huddled together, shoulder to shoulder. Then we extended our arms, and through touch and instructions we formed a square. It was a really good test of communication and working together, as well as being good fun. At the end of the exercise, we all happily removed our blindfolds, laughing our heads off when we saw the result of our work.

As we hiked back down, Kubra and I continued our conversation and Kate chatted with Nelofar. On the way back to the hotel we stopped at the "tank graveyard" in the field we had seen when we first arrived in Bamyan. Eight burnt-out Soviet tanks and troop carriers sit desolate in the field. In a strange way, they reminded me of when I was a boy and Dad and I used to assemble Airfix scale-model tanks and planes from the First and Second World Wars. But these were no toys. As I sat on the empty hulk of a tank, I thought about how it would have rolled towards Bamyan, ready to attack. I was hit with a wave of realization about the incredible events and violence this region had experienced: from Genghis Khan to the Soviet infantry.

It was late fall in Afghanistan, and so the heating was on in the hotel. Unfortunately, it was set quite high, and I'm not used to sleeping in a hot room. I tried to turn it down, but no luck. I didn't have a good night's sleep, again, and was awake at 1:30 a.m. on November 3, 2016: pre-race day. The heat had been a problem from day one, and management hadn't come up with a fix. I got up, opened the patio door and stepped outside. I looked up at the night sky and breathed in the cool night air. Then I went back to bed, thinking about my walk and talk with Kubra.

As I lay there, I thought about how much completing the marathon would mean to her, and I came to realize that maybe I could help her achieve her goal after all. What she lacked in training she more than made up for in mental toughness. I knew that if I ran with her there was a chance I could get her over the line before the seven-hour cut-off time. I decided then and there to have a talk with Taylor and Connie first thing in the morning. I would tell them Kubra deserved to have the opportunity to run the full 42.2 kilometres.

Despite having come to this resolution, no matter how hard I tried, I just couldn't get back to sleep. I went down to breakfast at 6:15 a.m. The place was deserted. I turned on the instant-drip coffee machine and waited.

SEVEN

SKATEISTAN

*"Imagine a bold plan for a world without
discrimination in which women and
men are equal partners in shaping their
societies and lives. Let's picture it!"*

– NICOLE KIDMAN,
UN Women Goodwill Ambassador

fter breakfast, Kate and I headed up to Colin and Liam's room
and prepared for a Skype call with Zainab. This was a very significant moment for me. Ever since I had read that article about her
in *The Guardian* a year ago I had been hoping to meet her. When I decided
to run in the Afghan marathon, I even hoped I would be running with her.
Unfortunately, Zainab would not be at the marathon this year.

At 8 a.m. on the dot, Zainab sent a note – "I'm ready" – and our video
conversation began. Zainab works for Skateistan, an organization that de-
velops sport opportunities for youth across Afghanistan. We chatted about
Skateistan for a while and then I told her about how inspired I was by her
work when I was recovering from my illness earlier in the year. In response
she said, "To me, running means freedom. I hope that at some point in
the future, all girls and women will be able to run without being harassed."

We signed off after chatting a bit longer, but I would go on to have more conversations with Zainab over the course of the year. What follows is her story, in her own words, written in 2017.

ZAINAB'S STORY

My name is Zainab Hussaini, and I was born in Iran, where I completed my first years of schooling with both boys and girls. Because my family were Afghan immigrants, my sisters, my brother and I were not given the same opportunities as the Iranian children. There wasn't any real opportunity to play sports until I went to middle school, when I joined a mixed basketball team.

At the age of 13, I moved with my family to Mazar-e-Sharif, Afghanistan.

I started learning Tae Kwon Do at a private sports club, but it wasn't long before the police came and closed it down because the club was not supposed to let girls take part in sporting activities. So a group of us decided to continue practicing at our high school.

After the Taliban regime ended, there was less risk in practicing, and we also played basketball. We were joined by some friends who had also returned from Iran. We formed a team and began entering competitions, always coming in second. I continued playing for four years, until I graduated.

In 2013 I went to work for Skateistan, an NGO that is the first international development initiative to combine skateboarding with educational outcomes. Although it started in Afghanistan, Skateistan now runs in Cambodia and South Africa too, reaching thousands of children and youth. Our mission is to empower children and youth through skateboarding and education, creating leaders that make a better world.

Through Skateistan I began training a team of girls to play basketball, and the team is still going, four years later. But it was a struggle. Fathers are not always happy about their daughters playing. By age 16, every girl on my bas-

ketball team had dropped out to marry. At first, I thought that I would have to do the same.

Luckily, in early 2015, I was introduced to Stephanie Case, founder of Free to Run, an organization that had been partnering with local schools to build a network of women's sport clubs, one at a time. But to cultivate local leaders for the long haul, it needed to motivate Afghan girls to push themselves to achieve what society said they couldn't.

One day, Stephanie asked, "Who wants to run an ultramarathon?" I didn't even know what ultra running was, but thought I would apply anyway.

I sent Stephanie a video of me, explaining about my Tae Kwon Do class being closed down, how I'd worn a burqa for three years (from the age of 13) and that during my time in high school I had been teaching young girls who had not been allowed to go to school during the Taliban regime.

When Stephanie saw my video, she selected me. Later she told me it was not for my physical ability but for my ideas and my courage. I felt so lucky. Five girls had applied, but only two were accepted: me and another Afghan girl, Nelofar.

We had never even run 1 kilometre, and now we had five months to train for the Gobi Ultra. We started running in the street, but, because of our lack of experience, we had no idea what we would face. On the very first day, we ran 10 kilometres, which was crazy, and we suffered a lot of pain.

There were also other issues to deal with. The worst was when, one day, a black car pulled up and tried to kidnap us. We managed to run away to a nearby shop. It was a really frightening experience.

After that, we stopped running in the streets, and Skateistan found us a club that had two treadmills we could use. But that didn't last long. After four days, some security guards at the club told us that they wanted to use them, at just the same time as we did.

We explained that we were training for a big race and that, if we did well, it would bring pride to Afghanistan. It made no difference. They weren't going to let us use them. So then we had to run around the yard at the Skateistan building.

On Fridays, which are holidays in Afghanistan, we would head into the hills *and run for between two and four hours. It wasn't easy, because although most people we encountered were good, there were also some who were drinking a lot of alcohol, which was a bit risky for us.*

On one of these runs, we found bullets and a mine, which we reported to the security services.

We often changed the places where we would run. There was a lot of bad public opinion about girls running. A male driver transported us to daily jogs and weekly trail runs, all under protective police watch.

To be able to take part in the Gobi Ultra, we need to obtain visas from the Chinese embassy. Unfortunately, at that time, Afghanistan was on China's blacklist, and they would not provide them for us. Fortunately, Stephanie had a contact who, through Facebook, asked for help and eventually they were granted.

At last, in June 2015, after all our months of training, we arrived in China and some Chinese ladies sang for us.

Experiencing the six-day ultramarathon was a very challenging chapter in my life. The first day, it snowed. I was very surprised to see snow in the desert. I slept in a tent for the first time, and that night it rained. It was so cold, and when I woke up in the morning I found my running shoes were full of water.

I was frozen, and by the end of the first stage I felt dizzy and was crying.

The second day was a mountain climb. Luckily, the weather had improved, and the sun was shining. Everything was going well until my feet began to swell and I developed blisters. I was in a lot of pain. I had to walk.

The third day brought more cold weather, and by the time I reached the first checkpoint, I was starving. I didn't like the food, but I had no choice and so I just closed my eyes and ate it.

That night, I was so tired when I crawled into my sleeping bag. When I awoke, on day four, I was soaking wet from the condensation, and the soles of my feet were really painful. I was also experiencing a lot of pain in my knee.

For the first few days, everyone had been inspiring and encouraging, but now Stephanie and the others were telling me to stop. At the time, it made me really sad. I couldn't understand why they weren't still encouraging me. It made me want to shout at them, but these were people I would know all my life and I didn't want one moment of anger and frustration to spoil our friendship.

At about nine o'clock that night, my spirit was gone because in my own heart I knew I had to stop. There were only 20 kilometres to go, and I felt so sad that I would not complete the run.

One of the team doctors rubbed some cream into my knee, took my hand and encouraged me to walk a little so he could assess what was wrong with it.

A journalist from London started to walk with me. We kept walking, and before I knew it, we had walked 10 kilometres. She kept telling me, "Zainab, you can do it." She was so positive, and she convinced me that, actually, I could.

In the early hours of the next morning, I saw the last checkpoint. Suddenly, I forgot all my pain and ran across the finish line. My friends were there, we were hugging and crying, and the sun was shining.

Despite having never run more than a few hours in the open, Nelofar and I had covered roughly one marathon per day over seven days. With Stephanie and Free to Run board member Virginie Goethals by our side, we had been chased through the desert by frigid snowstorms and blistering sandstorms under the weight of 20-pound packs.

At times, Nelofar and I, two Afghan women – one Sunni and the other Shia – knelt in prayer together in the rain.

When Nelofar and I unfurled an Afghan flag at the finish line of the 250-kilometre Gobi March, I felt like a winner because, to me, it was more than completing an ultra marathon, it was winning at life.

During the time I was running, with the snow and rain, the bad food and all the pain, I thought it was the worst experience of my life. I had told Nelofar that if I ever thought of doing something like it again, she had to remind me of just how hard it had been.

Two weeks later, I realized it had probably been the best experience of my life, and I wanted to do it all over again. I thank God that I was given the opportunity to take part. I felt I was one of the luckiest girls in Afghanistan, and I have a lot of people to thank, including RacingThePlanet, which organized the event, Stephanie and everyone who supported me.

I recovered well, and the day after arriving home, I went back to work. I became known in Afghanistan. People who heard about what I had done were divided into two groups. There were those who congratulated me and said "Well done" and were very supportive, but then there were those who tried to make problems for me and tried to ruin my reputation. They would be very critical of my personality, but I try not to let it bother me.

I was also attending university and some of my classmates, who are all male, congratulated me and said they were very happy for me, but others said they hated me for what I had done.

My family has been supportive right from the start. Although my mother did worry about me. Luckily, my father is very open-minded. He has even let me choose my own husband. Most Afghan girls don't even get to know their husbands before they are married.

My family is quite sporty. My father played football for 20 years, and my mother tells the story of when she was a girl, in Pakistan, she would run with her friends. One of her uncles would give a chocolate to whoever came first. My mother always won.

My brother, who is studying in Germany, is a boxer, and my younger sister, who is 23, sometimes ran with me when I was training.

I have two other sisters, both of whom are married and live in Iran.

Not long after Gobi, a friend of mine, who lives in Kabul and is leader of the Skyrunning club, told me that there was going to be a marathon in Kabul. It would be just one month after the ultra. I told him I wanted to run it and I would bring some other girls with me.

So Nelofar, two other friends and I went to Kabul and ran. It was an unofficial race and quite an adventure. People threw stones at us, and I asked myself whether I should have taken the other girls along. I felt responsible for their safety, and if anything happened to one of them, I would have had to answer to her family. In the end, we all finished.

In 2015 I received an email from Stephanie Case, inviting me to travel to Bamyan and take part in a marathon. I found it quite different to being in Mazar-e-Sharif or Kabul because it's at a much higher altitude (2743 m). I had one day to acclimatize and soon realized it just wasn't enough.

At the start of the race, I had problems with my breathing and pains in my chest. I had to keep stopping to catch my breath. Stephanie was running alongside me and encouraging me and telling me I'd done an ultramarathon, so I could do this. So I just kept going.

Along the way, many people who saw us were encouraging. A group of boys on their way to school ran a little way with us. But some were shouting bad things at us.

I wasn't sure of my finishing time, but I think it was around six hours.

Sadly, some male runners called me a liar and a cheat and wouldn't believe that a girl could actually complete a whole marathon. It turned out that the male winner had gone part of the way on a motorcycle!

When I went up to the podium, only five people were there to see me get my medal.

I was so proud. I was the only Afghan girl to ever complete an official marathon.

There was a lot of news coverage, many people in Afghanistan read about me and I received a lot of attention. Some people said very bad things about me on social media – even calling me a prostitute. But I felt that no matter what people said, good or bad, at least I had got their attention and I was bringing an awareness about girls and sport.

As a girl in Afghanistan, there is always a risk when you speak out. In March 2015, a horrific murder rocked Afghanistan. Farkhunda Malikzada, an educated Afghan woman and Koranic scholar, was brutally killed before a crowd of hundreds in downtown Kabul. She had argued with a man hawking charms outside a shrine about the piety of his profiteering and, enraged, he turned a mob against her. Video of the incident showed men and boys tearing Farkhunda's body apart with their hands, crushing her with a car and burning her corpse. Policemen stood watching.

I received the Franco/German award for Afghan 2016 Woman of the Year. Each year, the award is given for excellence in a different category, and that year it was for sporting achievement. There were many candidates. I was told I had been chosen because I had brought about change despite having to overcome many challenges.

The award ceremony was at the French embassy. The governor of Bamyan remarked that I would have been killed for running a marathon in other parts of the country. I gave a speech and talked about my plans for the future.

On receiving my award, the heads of both the cycling and basketball federations in Afghanistan challenged me and threatened to take me to court. They said I should not have received the award, and that I had only received it because I was the daughter of a diplomat. It was very upsetting. My father and my fiancé tried to speak up for me, but it had no effect, and so we had to just walk away. Eventually, a representative of the Afghan Olympic Committee intervened and explained that I was not related to a diplomat or anyone of great importance. I had been given the award because of the changes I had brought to the girls of Afghanistan.

They listened, and that was the end of the story.

Along with the award, I received 20,000 euros, which I donated to Free to Run.

I believe there are times in our lives when an opportunity comes along that is so unexpected, and we have to be prepared to take it, as something good can come of it and bring you great happiness.

I also believe that the future of Afghanistan is in our hands. We still have the presence of ISIS and the Taliban, but we must not allow them to force us to leave. Despite the challenges, we must continue to fight for change.

Skateistan is a mechanism that can enable that change. Working for the development of sports and life skills for children, it offers equal opportunities for everyone. The organization works with children from a wide variety of backgrounds – some from off the streets, some from single-parent families who may have a parent in prison, some who are not Afghan citizens and therefore not entitled to an education. In these cases, Skateistan provides participants *with a program to help them get accepted into public schools and to obtain ID numbers.*

Children are the future. They need to be taught about children's rights, women's rights, human rights.

At the time of writing this, I am in the third year of a four-year university course, studying International Relations, which is going very well.

I am also looking forward to being married and continuing in my work with Skateistan.

◇◇◇◇◇◇◇◇◇◇◇◇◇◇◇◇◇◇◇◇◇◇◇◇ SKATEISTAN ◇◇◇◇◇◇◇◇◇◇◇◇◇◇◇◇◇◇◇◇◇◇◇◇

In 2007 Australian skateboarder and researcher Oliver Percovich arrived in Afghanistan with three skateboards. He spent a few months in Kabul, talking to people about the attempts to rebuild the country after so many years of war. At the time, 70 per cent of Afghanistan's population was under 25, but Oliver saw very little investment in youth.

Oliver lent his skateboards to Afghan teenagers while he carried out his research activities during the day. The teens loved the freedom the skateboards gave them – they became the country's first skaters! When Oliver joined the crew later in the day and skated the streets of Kabul, he saw how the skateboards attracted youth from all backgrounds and genders – skateboarding had the power to bring youth together. An idea was born. Oliver started looking for equipment sponsors so he could bring more skateboards to Afghanistan. His idea became Skateistan, the first international development initiative to combine skateboarding with educational outcomes.

Oliver's programming began with skate sessions in Kabul in 2008, when he dedicated himself full time to his non-profit organization. Soon the organization was working on an indoor park, hiring local skaters and connecting skateboarding with educational opportunities. Skateistan provided not only skateboarding but also education – with equal amounts of skateboarding time and classroom time. Some children found themselves sitting in a class-room for the first time in their lives. By 2009 Skateistan was awarded NGO of the Year in Monaco, at the Peace and Sport Forum. Skateistan expanded yearly, running programs like Skate and Create (multimedia exchanges with youth in other countries), Back to School, and Youth Leadership (which included trips abroad for leaders), and opening another skate school in Mazar-e-Sharif. By 2012 Skateistan was reaching 400 children and youth per week with its programs. By 2016 Skateistan had programs in Cambodia and South Africa too, and its programming participants and leaders were 50 per cent female.

What started with a board and four wheels is now an award-winning, international NGO with the mission of empowering children and youth through skateboarding and education. Skateistan is creating leaders that make a better world.

◇◇◇

After hearing Zainab's story, I was keen to discover what some of the men in Bamyan thought about girls and women running in the race. Liam, Kate, Kausar and I headed out for lunch at a local *chaikhana*, where I spotted two men in another part of the café. I asked Kausar if he thought it would be appropriate for me to approach them and ask their opinions. He felt sure it would be OK and agreed to translate for me. He went over and talked to the men. He said they were willing to answer my questions and were fine with Colin and Liam filming the conversation. We went over and I established that they were both fathers of boys and girls. One of them supported the girls taking part in the race; the other said he had no issue with girls running but didn't like the idea of them running and taking part in a mixed-gender event. They did say they thought men in other parts of Afghanistan may not feel the same way, either because of a different cultural background or because of security threats to their regions.

As James Willcox notes in his story earlier in this book, Bamyan, because of its Hazara (Shia) population, is different culturally than the rest of

Sunni Afghanistan. These two fathers acknowledged this in our interview when they admitted that men in other parts of the country would likely frown upon girls and women running a marathon.

I was scheduled to give a presentation to the Free to Run Afghan women at 2 p.m., so Colin, Liam, Kate and I headed over to their hotel and located them in a small room at the back. I found it a bit strange talking to the group, which included Kubra. I hadn't told her yet of my plan, so in her mind she was still only committed to the 10K.

My talk covered the step-by-step process I always follow leading up to a race. What to do the day before, and then what action to take on race day.

It is critical to rest up the day before: don't do a lot of walking around and exerting yourself. Stay hydrated and have everything laid out the night before. What are you going to be carrying? Water, gels, electrolytes – have them ready. Race bib, shoes, socks – have them ready. Then, get a good night's rest.

On race day, have a good breakfast two hours before the race, and one hour before the race, drink a bottle of water. Get to the start line early and do some warm-up exercises. If it's extremely hot, wear a hat and white clothing, to reflect the sun. If it's cold, wear gloves and extra layers. Be prepared. When the gun goes off, start slow and finish fast. Don't get caught up in the start-line frenzy, you will soon be catching some of those runners who flew from the start line. Don't do anything new on race day. Do the same thing you did in training. Run for nine minutes, walk for one; this will get you through any marathon. At the end of the race, get some protein into you right away. A banana and chocolate milk work well. This is vital.

Finally, I emphasized that runners should always thank the volunteers. This prompted a question from one of the Afghan women: "If you're trying to come first, second or third, won't it take up too much time to say thank you?"

I said, "No, you can say it as you run. There's always enough time to thank the volunteers."

Afterwards I talked to Connie about my idea to support Kubra and help her complete the marathon. She was totally behind it, knowing I would be there to help if Kubra needed it. As soon as I had Connie's go-ahead, I left the room and headed off to find Kubra. She was in the hotel garden, taking a few moments for herself. I approached her and said, "Kubra, I've been thinking that if we ran together in the marathon we might be able to come in under the seven-hour limit."

She just looked at me.

I prompted, "So what do you think? I would be with you every step of the way."

She smiled then, and with tears coming down her face, she said, "Yes, I would like that."

Now both of us were smiling. We planned where we would meet in the morning and said goodbye.

The conversation with Kubra changed everything for me. The initial reason I had come to Afghanistan was to run and support the women and girls in their struggle for gender equality. I really hadn't thought about how I would run the marathon, but now I had a purpose: to help Kubra complete her first marathon.

EIGHT

MARATHON OF
AFGHANISTAN

*"All you need is the courage to believe in yourself
and put one foot in front of the other."*

– KATHRINE SWITZER,
American runner and first woman
to run the Boston Marathon

When *will I get a decent night's sleep?* My mind was going a million miles an hour. The conversation I had had with Kubra the day before was going around and around in my head. I was starting to question what I had done. Maybe the best thing would have been to have Kubra run the 10K race. What if we couldn't finish the race in time? What would the impact be on Kubra?

I lay in bed and watched as the clock hit 5 a.m. It was Friday, November 4, 2016. *Might as well get up*, I thought. By this point, I had come up with another one of my great ideas. I would wake Kate and together, on camera, we would prepare our water bottles with CarboPro, the race supplement I've been using for years. In my blurry state of consciousness, I was pumped about how amazing this segment would be!

My first task was to rouse Colin and Liam. I knocked on the door and Colin opened it. I said, "Morning, Colin, I have a great idea for a film segment: me and Kate preparing our race drinks."

Colin looked over at Liam and said, "Great idea. Let's do it."

Next, I knocked on Kate's door. She opened it and was not happy. I said, "Morning, Kate. would you like to shoot a segment of you and me making up our water bottles for the race?"

She just looked at me and said, "No, I'm going back to bed." Grumpy Kate told me to go away. So I did and returned to Colin and Liam's room. They filmed me preparing my water bottles. I used my Golden Tea Kettle, which I'd bought in the market, as the mixing vessel. It worked like a charm, and I couldn't help but hope that using the Golden Tea Kettle for this part of my usual pre-race process might bring me some luck.

After breakfast we all climbed into the van and soon found ourselves at the start line, in the shadow of where the big Buddhas had once stood. A French TV reporter asked if he could film me doing my pre-race warm up. I am not big on warm-up sessions; I'm just not the most flexible person. I did some moves for the camera, but I wasn't comfortable doing it.

Walking around the start area, I noticed a group of girls with scarves and toggles, and on their hats I read "Afghanistan Scout Association." One of the girls told me there were 30 girls in the Girl Scouts, 30 boys in the Boy Scouts and 50 children, both boys and girls, in the Cub Scouts. The boys met every Friday from 8 to 10 a.m., and the girls met from 10 to noon. "Some of us have been to a Jamboree," she said. I have all kinds of fond memories of being in Cubs and Scouts. We shared the Scout call, "Akela, we'll do our best!" Afghanistan is full of surprises.

I found Kate and we continued to mill around and meet up with other runners. Brad, Drew, Andre and Charlie were warming up, and Vicky, Paula and Irene were chatting with a group of schoolgirls. Off to the side,

Taylor and Connie were giving the group of Free to Run women and girls a final pep talk. Colin and Liam were shooting all the action as the clock counted down to the 8 a.m. start.

The whole thing was a sight to behold. There were a hundred runners, men and women, in the marathon and 150 in the 10K race, the majority of which were Afghan schoolgirls. Kate and I stood together. For a few moments we just took in the energy that exists at every start line – it was no different at this marathon start line in Afghanistan.

James Bingham then shouted out, "Ten minutes to the start!"

"Good luck out there, Kate," I said.

"You, too, Martin." She smiled.

She was wearing #261, the same number Kathrine Switzer had worn at the Boston Marathon in 1967. Actually, Kate's number was 61, but she had written a "2" in front.

◇◇◇◇◇◇◇◇◇◇◇◇◇◇◇◇ **KATHRINE SWITZER** ◇◇◇◇◇◇◇◇◇◇◇◇◇◇◇◇

Kathrine Switzer is best known as the woman who came up against the all-male tradition of the Boston Marathon. She was the first woman to officially enter and run in the event. But her entry in 1967 created an uproar when a race official tried to forcibly remove her from the competition. A photograph of this event became one of *Time-Life*'s 100 Photos that Changed the World.

After finishing the race, she was bent on making change for women. Alongside a sports marketing career, in which she encouraged others in both fitness and business, Switzer has run more than 39 marathons. She won the 1974 New York City Marathon, and in 1975 her 2:51 time at Boston was ranked sixth in the world and third in the USA in women's marathon. At this writing, she still runs marathons.

◇◇

Leaving Kate, I went to find Kubra. I had told her to meet me at the back of the group of runners, and there she was. She was wearing Nike running pants, a blue long-sleeve shirt with a Free to Run shirt over the top, a grey polka-dot scarf, striped hijab and sunglasses. She was ready. I said, "How do you feel?"

"I'm nervous but feeling strong."

"We'll let everyone else rush off and we'll stick to our plan," I said.

I could tell Kubra was excited and nervous at the same time. James Bingham began the countdown, and soon we were off! A group of runners shot off, hammering the first 500 m, but Kubra and I took it slow and steady. Kubra had agreed with my process: run nine minutes and walk one. Leaving the start area, we made our way along a gravel road. The other runners had kicked up a dust storm, and Kubra and I pulled up our running Buffs, covering our faces to avoid inhaling the dust. After 2 km, we left the gravel road and joined the main road.

For a while we ran with Mahsa and her husband, from Iran, and we proceeded this way until we reached the first aid station, at 5 km. Things were going well and we grabbed a drink of water.

At the 7-km mark, Colin and Liam caught up with us in the Filmmobile to record a conversation between Kubra and me. For the camera, we chatted about our progress so far and what it meant to be running together.

The climb was slow and steady as we continued to aid station two, at the 10-km mark. It was at this point that Kubra was hit with stomach cramps, so I suggested we walk for a while. The route steepened, and for the next 11 km we trudged up an incline. At the 18-km point, we met Kate coming in the other direction. We were thrilled to see her, and it was hugs all round. She ran with us hand in hand for 100 m, then said goodbye and headed off. For Kubra and me, that was a bright spot in a day that was turning out to be very challenging. We hit the turnaround aid station at the halfway mark and took a rest. The elevation at this point was 3139 m, and I was definitely feeling it.

Walter oversaw this aid station. He gave us each a banana and a cup of water. At this point, Kubra was struggling. We left this aid station at 3:36, and I knew we would have to pick up the pace if we were to come in under the seven-hour cut-off. I was starting to feel the pressure, and I really questioned whether we could make it. It was time to dig deep, and I offered her encouragement, trying to stay positive.

I said, "The wind is at our backs, the sun is shining, and best of all, we're heading downhill." With this, Kubra started running and the mental toughness I had spotted in her on the hike, two days prior, was coming to the fore.

Over the next 11 km our pace improved. Occasionally, we were shouted at by people standing at the side of the road. I asked Kubra, "What are they saying?"

"They are yelling 'Good luck!' and 'Run faster!'" she said, smiling. "Oh, and those three ladies we just met said we looked hot and tired. They invited us in for a cup of tea!" I don't think they really understood the concept of a marathon. Kubra managed a laugh. So did I.

As we ran/walked along, I encouraged Kubra to focus on our own race and not get distracted by other runners, let alone the people on the sidelines. A potential problem could have arisen if Kubra or I had become involved in a drama playing itself out near us. Two runners, who were going at the same pace as us, were having trouble coordinating their race. One kept running ahead and not listening to her partner, and the partner kept calling for the other to wait up.

I told Kubra, "We have to ignore them and stick to our plan." She nodded in agreement. I have to say she was a terrific student. She never wavered.

We reached the 32-km aid station at 5 hours, and I thought, *Yeah!* Things were looking good for the 7-hour cut-off. However, as we got going on the last 10 km, Kubra slowed down. Her lack of training was really starting to take its toll. I could tell she was having trouble, but she didn't complain. We ended up walking most of the 5 km to the 37-km and final aid station. By this point, we had only one hour until the cut-off. It would be tight.

As we pushed relentlessly towards the finish line Kubra told me, "One day, I want to be president of Afghanistan. When this happens, I will invite you to run a 10K, and we will have tea afterwards."

"That is an invitation I will certainly accept," I replied.

Kubra was breathing hard and her stomach hurt. She had taken a pain killer at the 32-km mark, but it hadn't kicked in yet. I checked my watch. We had 2 km to go, and we would have to cover it in 25 minutes. *We can do this*, I thought.

After walking in silence for some time, Kubra asked, "Can you see the Big Buddha?"

"No, not yet." But suddenly, with 500 m to go, I spotted the space where the Big Buddha had once looked out over the valley. We started to run in and could see the finish line. The area was full of people, and we had to push ourselves through the throng to cross the line. We did it, with a time of 6:52:27, just 7 minutes and 33 seconds inside the cut-off time. A volunteer put the beautiful medals around our necks. They were totally unique, made out of stone with the inscription "Marathon of Afghanistan, Bamyan Province, 4th November 2016" and bearing a picture of a markhor, a large, wild, spiral-horned goat found in Afghanistan.

Kubra broke down and started to cry. I gave her a big hug to console her. We were both overwhelmed. There were no words to describe how I felt, and I could tell that Kubra was not only greatly relieved to have finished but overjoyed at having made it.

I have run many marathons in my time, some faster than others. This was my slowest official time, but completing it with Kubra certainly made it one of the most memorable.

We parted, Kubra to get some rest and I to find Kate. This would be the last time I would see Kubra while I was in Afghanistan.

"Martin!" It was Kate. I saw her in the crowd and we made our way to one another.

"I was the third female in," she said. "I won the 'Third Lady' award!"

Kate looked great and her award was very cool. It was made of the same rock as the medals but was a plaque that you could stand up. The female awards were for First, Second and Third Lady.

KATE'S JOURNEY: THE SECRET MARATHON

Dust swirled around the runners' shuffling feet. Wherever I looked, excited faces peered back, eager for the race to begin. The early morning light glanced off the hollow caves where the big Buddhas once looked out over the mountainous Afghan city of Bamyan, before becoming target practice for the Taliban. Now only the ravages of war remained, that and the scene in front of me, the second Marathon of Afghanistan.

It felt unbelievable to finally stand here at the start line. I was decked out in my loose-fitting clothes, covered head to toe. An audio mic was taped inside my headscarf with the receiver clipped onto my running belt. My camera was on a short extendable stick, which I held in one hand. My running belt carried my four bottles of water into which my calories were premixed. These four bottles, totalling 0.7 L (or 3 cups) of water would have to last me the whole way. Salt tablets fit into another compartment, and my phone (also my backup camera) filled the final compartment. I had two running bibs on, my official number – 61 – on the front and my unofficial number – 261 – on the back. Kathrine Switzer's number. As I looked out at women in periwinkle-blue burqas cheering on young girls lined up to run in the 10-km race, I felt these women were carving out the same kind of path women like Ms. Switzer had carved for me.

The race was not without risk. We were told about the route only a week before the event and were sworn to secrecy to avoid being targeted by terrorists. Each person had taken a risk to be here. Armed guards lined the entire route and National Defense Service trucks followed closely behind each female runner, reminding us that this is a country is still very much at war.

The race followed a dirt path that merged onto asphalt. It started at 2500 m and climbed another 500 m up the mountainous desert region for the first half and then downhill for the second half. The air around me contained only 75 per cent of the oxygen I'm used to breathing, and I could feel my lungs gasping with every breath.

As I ran past the women in the race, we smiled at each other, each woman giving me a giant high-five and reaching out to hug me as I passed. Six Afghan women supported by Free to Run ran in the marathon along with seven women from other countries, 76 Afghan men and 11 international men. The men are as important as the women in this race because they have chosen to run alongside women. They are demonstrating that there can be a new way of understanding equality here in Afghanistan.

The constant uphill made my legs heavy, and I could feel myself slowing as though running through molasses. I thought of my friends, family and Leor, who trained with me. They were with me in spirit as I struggled up the hill. I kept going.

I was reminded of an African proverb: "If you want to run fast, run alone. If you want to run far, run together." In the past, I ran fast to outrun my thoughts, but now running far, I was building a community. Just as I reflected on this thought, a young Afghan man in his early 20s ran alongside me. "Do you mind if I run with you?" he asked. "I find it makes the time pass more quickly if you can talk with someone else." I smiled. The right person had come along just when the race seemed too difficult.

His name was Shekeb. He and I chatted, which did indeed make it much easier. He taught me new words, including ali, which means "excellent," and karhol magbul, which means "beautiful mountains." He ran with me for about 8 km and encouraged me to make it through the most difficult stretch of the course. He then spotted a friend behind us who needed some help, so I kept running on at pace by myself, determined to give this marathon my very best shot.

The downhill kept going, stretching on farther than any I had ever run before. As I pushed myself to go faster, there were long stretches where I was by myself to take in all the beauty. I saw my film crew, Colin and Liam, at two different stages, but I asked them to prioritize filming the other runners being featured in our film. I also noticed a white pickup truck that was always 100 m in front or behind me. I later learned it was the National Defense Service, tracking me to make sure I was safe.

Unlike on other runs, when I often must distract myself, I felt surprisingly calm and at peace mentally during the Marathon of Afghanistan. There was time to appreciate the beauty and soak it all in.

As I reached the final quarter of the race, I remembered an email I received from John at Viiz Communications: "A marathon is a 32-km warm up for a 10-km race." I began to feel what he meant.

That was when I met Najib. I shouted out, "Ali!" And he turned to acknowledge my praise. He slowed to allow me to catch up.

"Do you want to run together?" he suggested.

"I would love to," I said, "but don't let me slow you down."

He shrugged off my worry for his pace saying, "This race for me is all about having fun and coming together."

Najib and I kept running together and encouraging each other when one of us slowed down. He would yell out, "Come on, Katie, come on!" whenever I got too far behind, and in turn I would do the same for him.

Eventually, we caught up with an American runner named Bradley, who also joined our motley crew. About 2 km before the finish line, Najib suggested we should all join hands and cross the finish line together. Bradley and I happily agreed. Bradley was in the middle so Najib would not have to break custom and hold hands with a woman.

In the news, young Afghan men are described as terrorists and people to be feared. I had had two of such young men help me at the most critical points of my race. They both let go of ego and instead focused on the collaborative, collegial spirit of sport and having fun. Najib especially could have gone much faster but chose to stay with Bradley and me to finish with a symbol of unity.

Many people describe having a moment of pure emotion when they cross the finish line of a long race. They break down crying or they completely collapse.

For me, the race reminded me that I am not alone in life. So much of my life I have been afraid of not being good enough or liked enough or not being loved. I have let those fears dance circles around my mind until they trap me. This race reminded me that if I am willing to be courageous and take a few more steps in the right direction, I will be met by others who will share the journey with me.

I felt truly blessed as I crossed the finish line, hand in hand with an Afghan man and an American man. I came into this race scared that I would not be able to face down my own mental health struggles, and I emerged with a reassurance that I would not be left alone to face them. If I could keep moving, I would find the right person at the right time who would help me keep going a little longer.

For the next 30 minutes we circulated, congratulating everyone and taking photos. We were delighted to hear Colin and Liam say they had taken some great footage during the day.

As I finally headed over to the van, wanting to get back to the hotel and a hot shower, one of the international runners pulled me aside.

"You realize you just hugged a Muslim woman?" he asked.

I was taken aback. The thought that I should not have embraced Kubra after the race, in the way I did, simply because she is Muslim, had not crossed my mind. It was one human showing humanity to another. Kubra is a bit younger than my daughter, Kristina, and way back when Kris and I finished that 5K race together I gave her a big hug too. I thought about the two experiences – how proud I'd been of Kristina, and now how proud I was of Kubra.

We headed back to the hotel, where I had a cold shower. Not my choice, alas. This would be our last night in Bamyan, and I celebrated with a veggie pizza and a smoothie. An hour later, I found myself hanging out with Americans Drew, Brad and Mitch and Englishman Charlie. Charlie, an amputee, had run the marathon with a blade and come in second overall.

His leg had been badly damaged in a snowboard accident. He had had surgery and engaged in physiotherapy over a number of years, but his doctors couldn't save his leg. He told me he was planning to run races all over the world.

"Are you supporting a charity?" I asked.

"Yes," he replied. "Right To Play."

It was amazing to come across another runner so far away from home, running for the same charity I have been supporting for the past decade. One thing that struck me was how many runners are using their sport to help others. In 2013 I ran the London Marathon. It's interesting to note that this event holds the Guinness World Record for the largest single-day fundraiser. Races all over the world are helping a multitude of causes, showing that we can all make a difference.

◇◇◇◇◇ FILMING THE MARATHON OF AFGHANISTAN ◇◇◇◇◇

Colin and Liam agreed that filming the marathon was a highlight of their part in the filming process. They caught a variety of dramas throughout the day but were both taken by the power of the finish line. Colin said, "Seeing everyone cross that finish line and celebrate, seeing all that passion was unbelievable. And to see how everyone in the community was celebrating together ... so powerful!"

Liam later told me, "I captured a lot of celebratory moments, but I still remember seeing you, Martin, who everyone was waiting for, as you emerged near the finish line, with Kubra, who you had promised to run with. There was not much time left, but you two were running together. It was powerful to see the contrast of a first-time marathon runner and a seasoned marathon runner running together and making it to the end with each other's support." I have to say that I felt the same way!

◇◇

As we wrapped up our little party, James Willcox told us that the flight to Kabul was at 9:15, so we would leave the hotel at 8:15. I retired to bed and reflected on the day. It had started with a group of people – women and men, girls and boys, from different countries, religions and cultures – coming together for a common goal: to run a marathon or a 10K. It was a celebration of what we have in common, not an exercise in pointing out our differences. In the marathon, Kubra and I shared a journey. Learning from each other, we tried our best and achieved a goal.

They say you can never know a person until you walk a mile in their shoes. Well, Kubra and I had run 26.2 miles in each other's shoes and a bond had been forged that would never be broken.

Finally, on my last night in Bamyan, I was rewarded with a good night's sleep.

Meeting with Kate McKenzie and Scott Townend to discuss filming The Secret Marathon.
Photo courtesy of The Secret Marathon.

*With my daughter
Kristina at the end
of the Massey
5K race.
Photo courtesy of
Martin Parnell.*

Kart-e Sakhi Mosque. Photo courtesy of Martin Parnell.

The bread shop in Kabul. Photo courtesy of Martin Parnell.

Kate, in hijab, with Captain Clot-Buster at the end of the 2016 Edmonton Half-Marathon. Photo courtesy of Martin Parnell.

Local men giving rides to children on the hand-cranked Ferris wheel in a playground in Kabul. Photo courtesy of Martin Parnell.

The international runners arrive in Bamyan. Photo courtesy of James Bingham.

The cliffs in Bamyan in which the Big Buddhas, destroyed by the Taliban, once stood. Photo courtesy of Martin Parnell.

A burnt-out Russian tank in a field in Bamyan. Photo courtesy of Martin Parnell.

My running partner, Mr. Afghan. Photo courtesy of Martin Parnell.

Free to Run organizes a training run for some of the girls who will take part in the 10K race. Photo courtesy of Martin Parnell.

Colin and Liam filming at the caves. Photo courtesy of Martin Parnell.

Some of the boys who live in the caves. Photo courtesy of Martin Parnell.

The young teacher instructs her students at a school in a cave. Photo courtesy of James Bingham.

A mother and daughter display their beautiful handiwork at their store in Bamyan. Photo courtesy of Martin Parnell.

A group of Girl Scouts at the start line of the Marathon of Afghanistan and 10K races. Photo courtesy of Martin Parnell.

Runners line up at the start line of the 10K race. Photo courtesy of James Bingham.

Running with Kubra. Photo courtesy of James Bingham.

Mahsa and Kate at the finish line of the Marathon of Afghanistan. Photo courtesy of James Bingham.

With Kubra, at the finish of the Marathon of Afghanistan. Photo courtesy of James Bingham.

A lads' night out in Kabul. Photo courtesy of Martin Parnell.

Visiting my mum's grave, at Buckfast Abbey, Devon, with Sue, my brother Andy and my sister Louise. Photo courtesy of Martin Parnell.

Passing the baton to Gitti at TEDx YYC. Photo courtesy of Tony Esteves.

Celebrating with Wayne Benz at the end of the Dutchie marathon. Photo courtesy of Martin Parnell.

With Lana, Roy and Brett Ellis, setting up camp at the Golden Ultra in British Columbia. Photo courtesy of Martin Parnell.

Girls enjoying the Panjshir kayaking and camping trip, organized by Free to Run. Photo courtesy of Kristof Stursay.

Kids enjoy running the 2K Cookie Loop at the Eighth Annual Year-End Run/Walk. Photo courtesy of Martin Parnell.

Sahar enjoys learning to ice-skate in Bamyan. Photo courtesy of Taylor Smith.

With friend and fellow Right To Play athlete ambassador Hayley Wickenheiser. Photo courtesy of Martin Parnell.

Thanking John Wilson and James MacKenzie, co-founders of Viiz Communications, for their generous contributions to our film project. Photo courtesy of Martin Parnell.

Granddaughter and race director Autumn with her team for The Secret Marathon 3K, at the Running Room in Sudbury, Ontario. Photo courtesy of Autumn Beyers.

Free to Run organizes sessions for girls to learn to play ball hockey. Photo courtesy of Taylor Smith.

NINE

WOMEN AND GIRLS RACING IN AFGHANISTAN, 2016

*"Make the most of yourself by fanning
the tiny, inner sparks of possibility
into flames of achievement."*

–GOLDA MEIR,
teacher and fourth prime minister of Israel

Talking to people before and after the race, this much was clear to me: the stories of all the Marathon of Afghanistan runners – their lives prior to the race and how they came to be running that year in Bamyan – were fascinating. I asked two international female runners and four Afghan female runners to tell me their stories. The race has incredible significance for women's rights in Central Asia, but I found that whether the women runners were from the United States or Iran, Canada or Afghanistan – they all shared a dream for women's rights, equality and the freedom to run. Following are the stories of Taylor Smith (USA), Mahsa Torabi (Iran), Nelofar Sorosh (Afghanistan), Behishta (Afghanistan), Zahra (Afghanistan), and my running partner, Kubra Jafari (Afghanistan).

TAYLOR SMITH (USA)

The first time I heard the word "Afghanistan" I was sitting in my Grade 3 class-room in New England sometime after 9/11. It meant nothing to me. I remember thinking, How could a place I'd never heard of one day mean so much the next? *I never understood the fear that seemed to surround that word and infiltrate any room it was uttered in. I clearly still don't, as Afghanistan is now home. And what a home it is. In a country where the only consistent thing seems to be suicide bombings, there is so much life. Then again, Afghanistan has always been a place of extreme contrasts. Bustling streets and busy bazaars under the ever-watchful gaze of remote mountain peaks. A British cemetery filled with decaying graves occupied by those who made an attempt at taking Afghanistan over a century ago, adjacent to a polished memorial of more recent losses in the war on terror. Soviet silverware you can buy dirt cheap from a stall on the street next to a flashing wedding hall decked out in colourful lights. Armoured vehicles blazing through the streets past sooty street children and beggars missing limbs from encounters with landmines.*

I found myself in this ungovernable land, and subsequently at the start line of the Marathon of Afghanistan, through a series of snap decisions and fortuitous mishaps. The one constant through it all, though, has been running.

I grew up in an immigrant household surrounded by an Italian mother, grand-mother, aunt and, eventually, two younger brothers. Believe me, the need to run was always there. You really can't ask for better role models than three strong and stubborn Italian women who span three different generations, but you can ask for more personal time. Or you can try.

Nobody else in my family ran professionally, recreationally or even necessarily, so it quickly became a much-needed outlet and an easy escape route when there was too much pasta on the table or scolding coming from three mouths in rapid-fire Italian. But what started as an outlet transitioned into a mechanism for maintaining a sense of balance in my life. I can attribute almost every good habit I've learned over the last ten years or so to running. Self-control, perseverance, time management, critical thinking, you name it; it has roots in what I learned both on the track and on the trails.

Growing up in America, I mistook running as an inherent right. I didn't realize I was taking it for granted, until I found myself in Iraq. Recently graduated, I was having all the same anxieties and fears as my peers about finding a job and my place in the world. As if there is such a thing as "one right place" in the world. I applied for all sorts of jobs in all sorts of countries. One summer night, I sat at a bar with my boyfriend and a few friends, down by Fenway Park in Boston, debating two safe job offers in the United States and this wild job in Iraq. Something in me snapped.

An impulsive decision and an unexpected choice later, I found myself both single and living in Iraq. No longer could I step outside my door at any hour and go for a jog in shorts and a T-shirt. Women don't run in Iraq. Walking through the street alone will often result in harassment.

To run outdoors I would have to wear long sleeves and baggy pants, often with a male chaperone, or whichever poor friend I could con into braving the 38°C heat with me. Always, there was a constant ache and yearning in my heart for running free. I was training for a run across America in support of the Ulman Cancer Fund at the time, and through the countless hours I logged on the treadmill, I couldn't help but wonder if the women in this region knew what they were missing?

Curiosity piqued, I started digging around, looking for women's running organizations in conflicted countries. That's how I stumbled across Free to Run, the only organization I found that supports women running in conflict zones. And, oddly enough, they were looking for a country manager in Afghanistan.

Another snap decision later, I found myself in Afghanistan, going from the freedom of running back roads all the way from California to New York to a conservative society that disapproved of women outdoors even more than I had experienced in Iraq.

I got the answer to my question, though. Did the women in this region know what they were missing? Yes, they knew. And no, they wouldn't stand for it any longer.

Finding women and girls interested in sports, obtaining family permission for their participation, finding secure locations for them to practice. The list of obstacles goes on and on and on. Afghanistan is not a society that is ready to see women out jogging in the streets, even with a male chaperone. But the women of Afghanistan are ready. And who are we to deny them the freedom to be who they want to be?

My own Marathon of Afghanistan story is less inspirational and a lot more nerve wracking. I didn't sleep the night before, staying up stressing about what still needed to be done in terms of planning and preparation for the race and the million things that could go wrong.

I spent three hours before the race shepherding girls to the starting line on a bus in a panicked and speedy manner that I would argue resembled the aid distributions I had witnessed in Iraq. It was a constant stream of hands pawing at me for race bibs, Free to Run T-shirts, and the 20 sneakers we had on hand for over one hundred girls. Not enough gear, and not enough time.

All this combined with making sure our marathon runners from different provinces throughout Afghanistan, who had been training hard with us for months and were running the full marathon, were fully equipped and at the correct location. I almost missed James Bingham signalling the start of the race. I am also fairly certain I probably got in an extra 5 km that morning, racing around the city and schools to pick up participants.

Despite the chaos, I got it as I was flying up a dusty dirt road, flanked by two girls who would be the first two Afghan females across that finish line 42 km ahead. I could feel their energy pulsing off them as they pumped their arms with each stride. Behishta and Zahra were two of our youngest but fastest runners. With them positioned on either side of me, I realized that neither of them had ever known Afghanistan under Taliban rule. They didn't subscribe to the version of Afghanistan that would deny them access to education, force them into burqas and punish them for wearing nail polish. *Their Afghanistan was a world in which they could run outdoors. Not without threat or harassment, not the way I could exit my apartment and go for a run along the Charles River back in Boston, but a country in which they could run towards freedom. This was the first step, or rather the first 42 km, towards that freedom.*

Each step for them was a defiant declaration of true grit in the pursuit of freedom. And if you're looking for an example of just how tenacious they can be, try and give them an energy gel at the 30-km mark or convince them to pause for a drink of water at 35 km. The gel was aggressively spat out and cast off in a similar fashion to the photos of women removing their burqas after the Taliban fell. And I will never forget the feeling of fierce tugging, vehement head shaking and muttered, "Bia, bierem!" or "Come, let's go!" in Dari as I tried to pause for a brief sip of water. Left foot, right foot, dragging the American who wanted to pause for a drink behind them, they were making a statement. No man, woman, government, country manager or culture was going to tell them no.

However, the challenges of women running weren't going anywhere; they still haven't. As one participant crossed the finish line, her family would receive threatening phone calls that if they ever let their daughter run again, they'd live to regret it. Another would be forced off the road by a motorbike trying to run her over along the marathon route. Both are still running to this day. The problems in Afghanistan certainly aren't going anywhere anytime soon, but neither are these women and their commitment to being free.

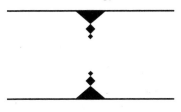

MAHSA TORABI (IRAN)

I am Masoumeh (Mahsa). I was born in northern Iran, in Gilan Province, in the city of Langrood, near the Caspian Sea. I grew up in an area where men and women work together. I grew up in a family where my father taught me how to bicycle and motorbike. My father always told me, "If you have a question, you can ask it. Please don't be ashamed of asking your questions. It is better to get an answer than remain ignorant."

Throughout my life, my father and mother have always been positive and encouraging about all my ideas, and they supported me in living out my dreams. One of my childhood dreams was to become the next Marco Polo. When I was a child, I watched Marco Polo on television. I saw that he travelled with his father and his uncle on the Silk Road. I told my parents, "I want to travel the Silk Road."

Today, I am a climber and have climbed many of Iran's mountains. I am also a cyclist, and I've travelled to many Iranian provinces by bicycle. At this time, I am working on research about the Silk Road in Iran, using my bicycle as transportation. Although I've been an athlete all my life, I only started running about one year before the 2016 Marathon of Afghanistan. I started running because the first international marathon race held in Iran would not allow women to run. When I learned this, I tried to get approval for women's participation in the race, but I wasn't successful. So, I decided to run in the first international marathon in Iran to show people women are capable of running a marathon. I wanted to show everyone that Muslim women can run with hijab. Nothing is impossible. In my mind, there are no limitations on what women can do.

After one month of marathon training and guidance from Free to Run's president and founder, Stephanie Case, I ran in the ultramarathon with her. We ran in the desert of Iran for 250 km. In this race, dear Stephanie taught me so many things, not only regarding sports but also my life. After that I became an ambassador for the Free to Run organization. That is one of my proudest moments.

It was so strange for other people when they heard I was training to run a marathon in Afghanistan. Many people told me Afghanistan is not safe for a woman. Some were worried about me, and some of them encouraged me and told me you are a brave woman for wanting to go to Afghanistan to run with girls.

When I saw many girls on the starting line, I was so happy and spoke with them and encouraged them in their running. I had very good feeling at the start line, and I was so happy Free to Run supported me and I could participate in a marathon race officially with other women and men. (Men and women together.) I ran alongside Alireza, my friend and supporter from Iran. When I met people on the route, I would smile to them and they would shake my hand. Sometimes I took photos with boys and girls who were cheering me along. There were cars with photographers and filmmakers and journalists who came to capture photos, videos and news. There were so many beautiful landscape views along the race route. We ran in the mountains, where there were many beautiful trees. We ran in nature as well as along an ancient route with old infrastructure along the way.

I ran the route, totally enjoying my race. I saw many young women during my run, and two or three times I stopped to speak with them and encourage them to continue with sports and running. They promised me they will be in the race again in the future. When I reached 21 km, I stopped for water and ate fruit and rested for five minutes. Then we were off again to reach the finish line. It felt good to see my friends along the route, and they encouraged me. At last we reached the finish line to the sound of cheers, photographs snapping, and a medal being placed around my neck. The feelings of joy never left.

When I ran in the marathon I reached a conclusion that there are no limitations for humans; only our thoughts can limit us. So I selected the name of "No Border Runner" for myself, and I now have a dream to run everywhere I like in the world. I will say to all women that they can run too, and I want to tell all women that they can follow their dreams. They can do everything they like.

Yes, the marathon changed my life. The race allowed me to find more friends from all over the world. And now I am sure and believe that nothing is impossible if women and men can run a race together in Afghanistan. I can do anything I want.

Afghanistan is a wonderful country, with the kindest people. This country has so much beautiful nature and beautiful history to explore. Afghanistan was one of the most important countries in the ancient time of the Silk Road. People in Afghanistan are hard workers and eagerly go towards learning by way of education. I think the race was a good opportunity for planting seeds of peace in this country.

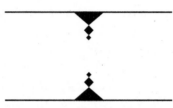

NELOFAR SOROSH (AFGHANISTAN)

My name is Nelofar. I was born and continue to live in Afghanistan. At this writing, I am 22 years old. In 2015 I was a part of the first team from Afghanistan to participate in the Gobi March, an ultramarathon in China. My family is an open-minded one that is always encouraging me in education and sport.

I started running in 2015 while I was working for Skateistan. After that I joined Free to Run, and then I was training hard because I knew that one day all my hard work and all my pain that I was feeling and all the problems I had would end and I would be proud of myself. I trained with Zainab, who was my partner in Gobi. We faced many problems when running in the community. But as I fought for my own right to run, I felt that I was fighting for the rights of all Afghan girls who are interested in sports but do not feel empowered to participate, as their communities and families do not allow them to practice or to enjoy sports.

The 2015 Gobi March (a 250-km multi-stage race) changed my life: it was my first-ever ultramarathon, first-ever running race and first-ever international experience. During the first stage of the race, I kept thinking it was all just a dream. The race had six stages, one per day, each requiring us runners to complete a certain number of kilometres. We ran the race despite pain, crying and blisters on our feet. I did not believe I would finish it. But along the way, I was always thinking about the cloth flag I had in my backpack. Afghanistan's flag. I focused on the finish line, thinking about how I would take Afghanistan's flag from my backpack (which I carried for the whole race) and run across the finish line with it. This was my dream for these six days, to show my country's flag to all athletes who participated in the race. I had a dream to show them all that we want peace and that we have Woman Power in our country.

Finally, after six tough days – six days full of pains and blisters – the race was over. We had made it. Zainab and I did not believe it, but we achieved our goal and we made the impossible possible.

Upon returning home, I participated in the Kabul Marathon organized by the local Skyrunning team. [Skyrunning teams the world over run and race at high altitudes.] I came in first place in the female category. I was feeling so strong and proud, and I found myself looking forward to participating in more races in the future.

I started a running club in Afghanistan through the support of Free to Run, trying to encourage other girls to experience the joys of running, which I had come to love. People's reactions were different when they heard that I was going to start running with girls in Afghanistan. Some were encouraging and proud that a girl would try to send a positive message, while others said it was not our custom for girls to do sports. After a few months of us training with the team, Free to Run sponsored us to run the official Marathon of Afghanistan, an international race in our own country. We couldn't wait.

When I reached the start line of the Afghanistan marathon, I was really excited, not only for myself but for many other girls who had come to the race from different places and from different nations. It was the first time I ran with our own Afghan girls who were new to sport. This motivated me and gave me energy at the start line – to see so many of our girls ready to run! I have never thought that running is easy, but when I saw my fellow Afghan female athletes, I felt so happy that I momentary believed that running is easy! Watching my girls participate in the marathon, and enjoy running as much as I did, made the whole race seem easy, and I smiled through the whole thing.

The race went well from the beginning. It was amazing. The first 10 km was easy, but after that, it was a bit tough. I kept going because I wanted to finish my first international marathon in my beloved Afghanistan.

Seeing the beautiful nature of our country and seeing our people encouraging us throughout the whole the race was really a different experience for me. I faced so many problems when practicing for my first ultramarathon and when we first started the running club, that I had come to expect the greater society's anger at me for running.

When I reached the finish line of the race, I was feeling very happy as well as excited. After several hours of running, and some walking and jogging, I found a result I was hoping for, but not expecting: a place in which I was proud of myself, a place in which I felt I was part of our society and serving our own people. Finishing this marathon was not easy, but I did it, and I achieved my goal with other Afghan girls by my side.

Before finishing the race and reaching that finish line, however, I was thinking about my family, because they were calling me every hour, asking me about my situation and telling me they were happy for me. They were proud because I was doing my part of being an Afghan and being a woman who is always thinking about her country and about gender equality in this poor country.

I met many people who were living along the marathon route who were new to the idea of a marathon. Their curiosity and questions encouraged me to keep running and to continue in this work. Meeting the international runners along the way was very interesting as well, and they kept encouraging us throughout the race.

Life after the marathon has been interesting. Many changes have come to my life since finishing the marathon in Afghanistan. I was energized by it, and it motivated me to move forward and ahead with my life. I have decided to continue along my path, all the way through to the end of my life. After all, sport is something that keeps people hooked and interested; when you get in the habit of running, you can never quit running. This marathon helped me increase my self-confidence, and it helped me know that I should never quit running in my country, no matter what.

I am hopeful for women in Afghanistan, despite the challenges we face in achieving our goals. After running the Marathon of Afghanistan, my family received several threatening phone calls from the community, telling them to never let me run again. But my family supports me and our team to continue.

Running has changed my life, and I believe anyone who runs a marathon will feel that the marathon is a life-changing thing. It's a tough task, and you will realize how powerful and energetic you are by finishing it. In running a marathon, you will find your life's path, just as I found mine.

Through running, I have realized that nothing is impossible in my life if I try my best from my heart, if I use all my power to do it.

Afghanistan is a country where you do not see many women, not only in running or other sports, but anywhere. Every female who starts running or taking part in any other sport will face many problems because our people are new to the idea of sport and they don't know about women's rights in sport. When Afghan women and girls struggle for their rights to sport, they encounter lots of problems, and it will take time until our people realize and understand the positive aspect of having girls involved in sports.

In the meantime, we are the females who can change our country and who can change the minds of our people. We know it will be hard and it will take time, but we should not quit. We should motivate other Afghan girls who are struggling for their rights in our country because they need our help to do it. We are here to help each other and to bring positive change through sports to our beloved Afghanistan.

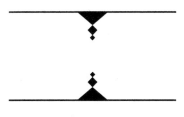

BEHISHTA (AFGHANISTAN)

Hello, I am Behishta[2] and I am 16 years old. I live in a small family. I have been interested in sports forever. Teacher Nelofar was our teacher in Skateistan. One day she let us know about Free to Run, and I became very interested. I have been practicing with Free to Run for almost a year and a half. During this

2 I have changed this young woman's name to Behishta to protect her privacy.

time, I have finished a marathon and a 10-km run. My first half-marathon, my first 10-km run and my first 5-km quick run happened after months of practicing. And I did the Marathon of Afghanistan with my teammates after a year of practicing.

The Marathon of Afghanistan was my first out-of-province marathon. I was so nervous before the race. I was wondering, How can I come in first and beat all the foreign runners who seem stronger and better than me? I hadn't had enough sleep for nights, and I kept going to my early morning practices; during all these times, all I wanted was to come in first. A few nights before the race, most of our teammates were getting sick, so I was also scared to get sick and not make it to the race. I was trying to take care of myself and not get sick. Teacher Nelofar was taking care of our food and our drinks as well. And she continued to guide us. I had a good week before the race during which I found new friends, and everyone was treating us the same as everyone else.

Zahra, Ms. Taylor and I were teammates during the race. The unity of our team and our speed were good, and Ms. Taylor kept helping and encouraging us. I tried hard to come first, but some obstacles prevented me. Some strangers yelled at Ms. Nelofar and threatened her, trying to make her give up on the race so none of our teammates could win any awards. But Ms. Nelofar kept running, and she didn't stop. I got a bit ahead of Ms. Taylor and Zahra. On the way, some people showed me the wrong way, but luckily I found the right way again soon. After that, some other people hit me with a motorcycle, and I got a bit injured, but I kept running.

I remember Ms. Taylor and Ms. Nelofar telling us not to get separated from the team because we would get into trouble and they wouldn't be able to take care of us, but I wanted to come in first, so I ran faster and got separated from my teammates. Later on, I understood my mistake. If I hadn't gotten separated from the others, I could have finished the race comfortably and easily like Zahra did, and nothing would have happened. But it was still an experience, and I am happy I learned from it. I learned that I should listen to my teachers. Although I faced a lot of problems, I enjoyed it. I was happy about it and I felt strong.

After the race was over, we all got medals. I came in fourth among all the female participants. I was happy about the fact that I got a medal, but I was sad at the same time, thinking about all these problems that had stopped me from coming in first. But I still have hope, and I want to finish first next time.

After the race, everyone came to my home to see me and congratulate me. Some people praised me by giving gifts. Even in my school, everyone was celebrating the race with me. I have become famous at school, and now everyone wants to be my friend. Some of them ask me to join their teams. I am happy. Free to Run gave me this chance to have new experiences, make new friends and have all these memories. I want to thank Ms. Taylor, Ms. Nelofar, Stephanie Case, the supporters and everyone who has been working and helping out with this program. Thank you, everyone.

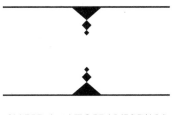

ZAHRA (AFGHANISTAN)

My name is Zahra[3] and I am 15 years old. I was so interested in sports that I joined Public Health soccer through a program. And from there I joined Free to Run, and I became interested in running. As I write this, I realize it has been almost a year and a half that I have been working with Free to Run. I have completed one marathon and a half-marathon race during this time. My first competition was after months of practicing. Completing a 10-km race, a 21-km half-marathon and the Marathon of Afghanistan happened after a year of practicing.

I was so nervous because it was my first marathon. I thought, It will be very difficult. *But, we went to a practice with Ms. Taylor. She taught us a lot of things, such as how to help each other when we get tired during the race. We had*

3 I have changed this young woman's name to Zahra to protect her privacy.

another small meeting with Mr. Martin, where he told us what to eat during and after the race. I learned a lot of things such as teamwork, helping each other, and how to be friends with my new friends there. Although I was nervous before the race, I was happy about the fact that people from different genders were competing against each other. We were looking at each other not through our genders, but through a different lens, that of humanity. I was feeling comfortable. It was unbelievable that it was possible to have such a situation in Afghanistan.

Everything was surprising, and it felt like Afghanistan was somewhere else. I can't tell you how pleasant and memorable it was. It was one of the best memories of my life. I was scared that if I couldn't finish the race my family would say, "You lost because you are a girl and you are weak." But Ms. Nelofar kept encouraging me, and she kept saying that I can finish way longer races than this, and all I need is to be confident and to believe in myself. She was like an older sister to us, and she helped us a lot.

Ms. Taylor and I were on the same team during the race. Although it was my first time running with her, and we didn't understand each other's languages very well, I learned a lot of things from her, such as teamwork and helping others. She was so kind. While we were running, it was unbelievable for me to believe that people were racing each other on the streets of Afghanistan, a country where people have been living with fear of bombs for years and no one knows what will happen in the next hour.

We were all so comfortable, enjoying every single moment. I wasn't feeling any pain and I wasn't tired either. Sometimes we were joking with each other. Whenever we passed a checkpoint, I remembered Ms. Nelofar saying that we needed to help each other and stay with each other. I found a lot of new friends, especially Ms. Taylor, without whom I couldn't have completed the race as well as I did.

At the end of the race when I got a medal, I was so happy, and I was more confident. Whatever Ms. Nelofar had said would happen was happening. I wanted to tell everyone in this world that I had finished the race and my dream had come true. Later on, we had a meeting in a hotel where we all talked about our experiences with each other.

I learned to be nice and kind to people and make new friends. And that night, until late, I was talking to my friends, telling them about my marathon. After I got home, my family and all my friends were waiting for me with flowers and gifts. We had a small party in the house as well. Everyone, including my teammates, encouraged me. I hope I see my friends once again and refresh all the memories.

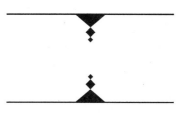

KUBRA JAFARI (AFGHANISTAN)

I was born in Tehran. My family had to leave Afghanistan, and we were living in Iran, as refugees. My father had no permanent job but worked on farms, looked after cows, and did some masonry. My mother also worked, and I began working, at the age of seven, picking fruit, helping on farms and weaving carpets. I was also going to school. I have a sister who is older than me by two years and two younger brothers.

My parents were given permission to send their children to a government school. There were both boys and girls in my class, up to Grade 5. I didn't have any opportunity to take part in sports, but we would play games like Chase. I loved reading and had many books of short stories. When I was in Grade 4, I donated some of them to the school and set up a small library. I remember my first book was Pinocchio. *I attended up to Grade 7, but then my parents were told they would have to pay if they wanted me to continue, but they couldn't afford it, so I had to leave.*

My father wanted his children to have an education, and so he decided to take us back to Afghanistan, where we settled in a district of Kabul. By this time, I was 14 years old and had missed a year of schooling, so I went straight from Grade 7 to Grade 9.

The lessons weren't difficult, as the standard of education was lower there than it was in Iran. I wasn't happy at my new school. The teachers and children mocked us because of our accents and clothes, and said, "Stay away from those Iranians." It was very hurtful.

I didn't have much to do as, each day after school, I would go home and weave carpets. But, I was very happy to find a good bookstore and continued to pursue my love of reading. One book I remember specifically was How to Win Friends and Influence People, *by Dale Carnegie.*

After living among the fields, fruit trees and green countryside of Tehran, it was strange to be in the mountains of Afghanistan, where there was hardly a tree to be seen. In Iran we had electricity and good food and water, but not in Kabul. For about a year, my family kept getting sick.

My goal was to learn English, go to university and obtain my PhD. Unfortunately, despite studying very hard, I failed the entrance exam for the university of my choice. Instead, I applied for a scholarship to study, for seven years, at the Asian University for Women (AUW) in Bangladesh and was accepted. But I couldn't settle and found it hard to adapt to the hot climate and the food, and I became very homesick. Eventually, I decided to leave and return to Kabul.

My mother was working, weaving carpets. My father didn't like Kabul, and so he was travelling back and forth to Iran for work. He would send money home for the family. My sister was married by this time, and so it was just me and my two brothers at home with my mother.

After Bangladesh, I was extremely depressed and didn't know what I was going to do.

One day, my best friend took me to an education centre and showed me a computer program called Premiere Pro, which is a video-editing software package suitable for both amateur enthusiasts and professionals. For three months, I learned how to edit films and then I got a call to say I'd been accepted for the Youth, Solidarity and English Language program (YSEL), at the American Embassy in India.

Administered by American Councils for International Education, the Youth,

Solidarity and English Language program is a month-long, English-immersion academic camp for secondary-school-aged students from different provinces throughout Afghanistan. In addition to English-language-acquisition, the program cultivates a strong sense of national identity, youth solidarity, leadership and volunteerism.

It was then that things really began to come together. I studied hard and learned so many new things. All the teachers were American, and I became aware of a world, outside of my own, that I had known very little about. It gave me hope and made me realize that, despite all that had gone on before – not getting into university, my time in Bangladesh – that was in the past, and I now had the opportunity to achieve many things.

I started volunteering with children and was chosen to go back to India for a year and work as a counsellor for YSEL. After that, I spent six months making documentaries for Afghan Voices, a content-development program.

I met a businesswoman who introduced me to Peace Through Business, a business training and mentorship program for women entrepreneurs in Afghanistan and Rwanda. The program is in its 11th year and is implemented through three major components – In-Country Education, Leadership Development, and Pay It Forward – which combine to create a sustainable program to educate women, promote their business and leadership skills, build a strong public-policy agenda in the women's business community, and help build stable democracies.

I made a proposal to them, explaining that I would like to create a business making documentaries, animation and advertisements relating to the protection of females. They liked my idea and I was chosen to go on a three-week trip to America, to learn about entrepreneurism. I spent two weeks in Dallas, Texas, and a week in Oklahoma. I liked America, but the trip was spoiled when some of the women on my team ran away.

The organizers were afraid that the four of us remaining would do the same, and so we were then watched very closely all the time. It was a shame. There I was in the country of freedom, and yet I felt like I was in a prison.

I returned to Kabul and continued at university. In the end, I decided not to pursue my idea for a business relating to protection and, instead, by January 2015 had set up two other businesses. One was a planning business for celebrations such as birthdays, weddings, graduations and so on, and the other was a business that designed shopping bags for stores – I would travel to Iran to buy the materials.

In the spring of that year, I was introduced to Stephanie Case from the NGO Free to Run. She was looking for a videographer to accompany her on a trip to film two female Afghan athletes, Zainab and Nelofar. On our return, I continued to film them at home, at work, training on the treadmill and in the mountains.

As I watched them, I felt a part of me was missing. I wanted to run too. They had inspired me.

I started running on a treadmill and told Stephanie that I wanted to join the next group to run an ultramarathon. She sent me an application, which I completed, and I persuaded my friend Arzoo to fill one in too. She had never run, but I told her she'd enjoy it.

We were so happy when we found out we'd been accepted for the Racing-ThePlanet Sri Lanka Ultramarathon. Training on the treadmill was hard, so we would go out onto the empty streets at 2 a.m. and run. At these times, Arzoo said she felt liked the streets belonged to us, and that freedom to run gave her power.

One morning, a guy cycled across my path and hit me, and sometimes, when we went hiking, people would look at our hiking gear and sports clothes and harass us, saying we were "not good Afghan girls."

I had a very difficult time at the race. At first things went smoothly, but at around the 30-km mark I had a panic attack and had to drop out. But I did stay and volunteer for the rest of the event. Arzoo finished the race but afterwards decided she didn't want to run anymore, and she quit. Although I hadn't achieved my goal at the ultra, I knew it wasn't the end for me.

I wasn't going to give up, as I still felt I could be a good runner, so I kept on running. I asked Stephanie if I was still on the team, and she said I was. I loved that.

My next race was the Bamyan marathon, on November 4, 2016. I remember, on the day, feeling really scared, but once I got going, I told myself I could do it. Things got really messy around the halfway mark, as I hadn't trained properly. It was a very strange feeling because I was telling myself, Just keep going ahead, *but my body was saying,* No, you can't do it. *When I reached the finish line, it was an awesome feeling that I had achieved something. It's a feeling I will never forget. I know I couldn't have done it without the support of Martin Parnell, a runner from Canada who helped me get through it. He encouraged me the whole time and never let me get my spirits down.*

After the marathon, I returned to Kabul and started working for Free to Run on a part-time basis. I was also working at FKH Media Productions, as an assistant project manager. The company produces high-quality media products and public-outreach services and undertakes commercial and public-awareness campaigns throughout Afghanistan.

I took part in a four-day hike and kayaking expedition for girls in the Panjshir Valley. When I returned, my manager at FKH gave me a warning, even though my boss, who operates out of Turkey, had given me permission to go. I Skyped with my boss and explained that I didn't think it was fair and, also, the fact that the manager had told me he hadn't wanted a girl working there and was against me being hired. Unfortunately, the boss said he couldn't go against the manager's decision, so I resigned.

Around that same time, my mother had decided to take my brothers and return to Iran. Everything was so mixed up. I was in a very tough situation. I'm so glad that I had my running. I would run three times a day. I had my teammates, and they made me feel better and stronger.

Since July 2017, I've been employed by Free to Run on a full-time basis and, at the time of writing, I am working with them to prepare for the third Marathon of Afghanistan in Bamyan in late October 2017. I am planning to run again and, this time, I want to be the first female finisher.[4]

I have just graduated from university and, next year, I hope to begin working

4 *Kubra finished the marathon in 5 hours 30 minutes. Even though she wasn't First Lady, she beat the time she set in the 2016 event by over 1 hour 20 minutes.*

towards my master's degree. I was one of a group of five Afghan women who made a presentation to the UN, at its compound in Kabul. After that, I went to Bamyan to learn ice-skating and I met up with Zainab and Nelofar.

I have told Martin that I have dream. One day, I am going to be the president of Afghanistan and I will invite Martin to come and visit me. We will drink tea and go for a 10-km run.

That is still my dream.

TEN

WINDING DOWN

*"Learn from the mistakes of others. You can't
live long enough to make them all yourself"*

– ELEANOR ROOSEVELT,
American politician and activist

I t was the morning after the marathon. I'd had another restless night,
most likely a reaction to the marathon. I often find, after a long race,
I experience some muscle spasms in my calves and quads. We took
an early flight to Kabul and were then returned to the Cedars, the same
guesthouse we'd stayed at when we first arrived.

I was exhausted, and so was everyone else, but after a cup of tea, we
headed into the city. Tired as I was, I wasn't going to miss visiting the
British Cemetery. This quiet place, tucked behind high wooden doors
and a fence, is also known as the White Cemetery. This cemetery was
established in 1879, after the Second Anglo-Afghan War, replacing the
cemetery set up during the first war. Some of the stones date back to
1842. But the gravestones don't only document British soldiers who died
on Afghan soil. Laid to rest in this quiet corner of Kabul are foreign aid
workers, engineers, explorers, journalists, missionaries and soldiers from
other countries. Each stone represents decades of Central Asian history,

and the foreigners who came to exploit, to help, to defeat and defend, some simply to travel and find out more about Afghan culture and its people.

The Taliban wreaked havoc on this place during its time in power. Many stones were vandalized or ruined, but the cemetery's local caretaker, Rahimullah, did what he could to restore the place after the regime fell. At this writing, Rahimullah's son, Abdul Sami, is the curator.

I slowly walked around, looking at the gravestones and commemoration plaques. On the walls were tributes to Australian, New Zealand and American soldiers. I was saddened when I noticed the plaques for the Canadian soldiers who served in Afghanistan had not been installed and were lying on their sides on the ground.

That day the history of war turned out to be a recurring theme. After our quiet reflection time in the cemetery, we visited a carpet shop, where we sat around and listened to the merchant tell war stories. He had been part of the mujahideen and fought the Soviet army. Being in the shop had a strangely soporific effect, even with the carpet seller's stories of battle. I began to doze off and only awoke when the man began throwing carpets on the floor for us to look at. I shook off the drowsiness and joined a group that were moving farther down Chicken Street. James Willcox took us into a store that had several rooms. It was stacked full of scarves, coats and hats. I tried on a hat that made me look like Hamid Karzai, a former president of Afghanistan.

On the final night in Afghanistan I had the best sleep on the trip so far. The room was cool and the duvet was warm. The next morning, I had a chance to chat with Kate.

I said, "Kate, you've completed Part One of the plan! You trained hard, ran the marathon and came in Third Lady!"

She laughed.

"Now," I said, "it's time for Part Two."

Kate had told me that her future goal was to qualify for the 2018 Boston

Marathon. But to do that, she really needed to participate in a couple of 10-km races first, then a half-marathon, and then in September 2017 run a qualifying time at the Toronto International Marathon, which would allow her to apply for Boston. We also discussed her other goals, especially completing the documentary film and raising awareness about women and girls having the freedom to run.

As Kate and I were talking, Colin walked over and asked, "Did you hear? There have been riots in Istanbul."

He had heard that protesters were demonstrating against the recent arrests of pro-Kurdish lawmakers and journalists who sympathized with the Kurdistan Workers' Party (PKK). Police were cracking down, hard. Tear gas was being sprayed, batons were being used liberally on crowds, and arrests were being made, making Istanbul a very unsafe place. This was just one more step against democracy in Turkey since President Recep Tayyip Erdoğan had vowed to squash "enemies of the state" after a coup attempt. His actions had resulted in dissenting military officers, teachers and public servants being fired and whole media organizations being shut down. The Kurds, long-time critics of the government and fighters for equal rights, represent Turkey's largest ethnic minority, and Erdoğan was cracking down on them most of all.

Colin, Kate and I exchanged a few worried words about the situation in Turkey, but James Willcox was on top of it. "The riots are not affecting the airport," he said. "We'll be able to proceed."

After a couple of hours relaxing in the very sparse business-class lounge at Kabul Airport, the call went out for Turkish Airlines TK707 and we boarded.

When we landed in Istanbul, I said goodbye to the group. They all had a six-hour layover. Fortunately, mine was only two hours. Before long, I was boarding the Lufthansa flight to Frankfurt and heading back to a more familiar part of the world. My flight to Calgary did not take off until the following afternoon, so I had booked myself into the Airport Sheraton, where I took advantage of the steam room, which set me up for a good night's sleep.

I slept well, but, like clockwork, woke at 6 a.m.

I turned on the TV and an Italian news station was showing live coverage of the New York Marathon. It registered with me that, only two days previously, I was competing in a marathon too. Somehow, that event felt like it had happened so long ago. Afghanistan's marathon and New York's race are two very different animals. In the NYM there is huge prize money for the winners of the men's and women's races. In the Marathon of Afghanistan, the top three men and women receive plaques and jackets. In the 2016 NYM, 20,696 women finished the race, the most in that event's history. In the second Marathon of Afghanistan, 13 International and Afghan women finished.

I turned the sound down and watched the race unfold from the halfway point. The men's winner was Eritrean Ghirmay Ghebreslassie, at age 20 the youngest man ever to win. The women's winner was Mary Keitany of Kenya. She became the third woman to win the NYM three times.

In my attempt to catch up with world events, I wandered down to the newspaper kiosk to pick up some English-language papers. I bought copies of *USA Today*, *The Wall Street Journal* and *The New York Times*. Page after page was devoted to the coming US election. However, the *Times* also carried a front-page article on Afghan refugees returning, supposedly voluntarily, from Pakistan to Afghanistan. These were some of the internally displaced people we had talked to during our visit to the caves in Bamyan.

Even there, in a hotel in Germany, I was caught by headlines that took me back to Afghanistan. As I was getting ready to check out, I was watching CNN and there, at the bottom of the screen were the words "Australian woman kidnapped in Kabul." She was working for an international aid organization, the Agency Coordinating Body for Afghan Relief and Development (ACBAR), which brought together more than 146 NGOs operating in Afghanistan. It wouldn't be until the spring of 2017 that this woman would be released by her captors.

The flight from Frankfurt to Calgary was incident free. I went through the Air Canada inflight entertainment and watched episode after episode of the BBC serial *The Night Manager*, based on the John le Carré novel. In it, I found some escape from the thoughts whirling in my head.

As we neared Calgary, I became concerned about the customs process. Would I be grilled about why I had visited Afghanistan? I thought back to 11 days ago when I checked in and was asked, "Are you going to join ISIS?" My fears were soon laid to rest. We arrived at the new international terminal, and everything was automated. I had my passport and declaration card scanned, and I was on my way. No questions as to where I'd been or why I had been there.

Driving home from the airport, I couldn't help but notice how good the roads were compared to the ones we'd travelled on in Afghanistan. With the air conditioning on and CBC on the radio, the drive seemed to take but moments, and I was soon parking in the garage. I walked into the house, and Sue was there to greet me.

It felt so great to be back in the warmth and comfort of our home. I could tell how happy and relieved Sue was that I had gone and come back safe and sound. We'd both missed each other, but I'm very aware that whereas I was caught up in all the excitement of the trip, for Sue it was more a time of waiting and worrying. It's often harder for the person who stays behind.

My incredible Afghanistan adventure was over.

Now it was time to begin processing all that I had experienced.

ELEVEN

NEXT STEPS

"Whatever happens next, I'm sure
it's going to be a great adventure."

– JEN CALONITA,
author

y trip was over, but there was still much that needed to be done. I had decided to dedicate my Seventh Annual Run/Walk, at the end of December, as a fundraiser for Free to Run. Before leaving Afghanistan, I had spoken to Taylor about the possibility of raising enough money to build a new volleyball court at the school we had visited. There was plenty of work to be done on the film, and I wanted to find other ways to support the women and girls in Afghanistan.

A couple of days after returning home, I received an email from Kubra. In it was a testimonial detailing how she felt about the marathon:

42k, 10k, half-marathon, or ultramarathon: it does not matter which one. This is all about your mind, it is a fight between your mind and your body. If your mind is ready, no matter what, your body will keep going in all steps.

I was lucky to learn this lesson from a great man of inspiration, Martin Par-
nell, who did 250 marathons in just one year. He told me I have a strong mind
and I can do the Bamyan marathon as my first marathon though I did not have
enough training.

How can I express my feelings? That moment, when you cross the finish line,
that moment is a golden time that not everybody can experience. I have been
given this chance two times, once during the Sri Lanka ultramarathon and once
in the Bamyan marathon. It would have been impossible if Free to Run did not
provide me this opportunity. The opportunity to know more about my strengths,
my weaknesses, my own mind, and to feel real freedom through observing and
connecting with nature while running.

Now, I run to earn the street and open it for my daughters and granddaughters.

Reading this ushered in a flood of emotion. She thanked me for helping
her finish the race, and as I was reading her words, all I could think about
was how I wanted to thank her: for her strength and for the honour it was
to have met such a strong person in such a difficult place for women to
flourish and thrive.

A week later, Kubra and I Skyped. The connection was terrible, and
though we tried to connect a few times, the call kept getting dropped. Finally, we were able to speak for about five minutes. We chatted about how
she was feeling and what she was doing. I was thrilled to meet her mother
and her brother, Amir Abbas, who is four years old.

That same day, as I started thinking about what needed to be done
next, I received a message from Leanne Brintnell, an event coordinator
who volunteered with the Calgary chapter of an organization called Canadian Women for Women in Afghanistan (CW4WAfghan). She wrote,
"This morning, while drinking my morning coffee, I heard your name on
the CBC morning show. I have been a keen follower of your story since

reading the *National Post* write-up on your marathon run in Afghanistan. After reading this story, I made a note that I should contact you in the New Year. Hearing your name this morning and hearing about your fundraising initiative to build volleyball courts in Afghanistan made me so excited that I decided I needed to reach out to you right away."

CW4WAfghan turned out to be a community of citizens throughout Canada who contribute to advancing education for Afghan women and girls. Leanne wanted to meet with me to discuss our common interest in Afghanistan. She wanted to be part of my volleyball initiative somehow, and she also wanted to introduce me to CW4WAfghan's Students in Action group, which was interested in helping with the Seventh Annual Run/Walk fundraiser!

◇◇◇◇◇◇◇◇◇◇◇◇◇◇◇◇◇◇ CANADIAN WOMEN ◇◇◇◇◇◇◇◇◇◇◇◇◇◇◇◇◇◇ FOR WOMEN IN AFGHANISTAN

In 1997 Calgarians Janice Eisenhauer and Carolyn Reicher met at the University of Calgary. They were both shocked by the human rights violations Afghan women were facing under the Taliban regime, and they began to explore how they could effectively help Afghan women. This is how the uniquely Canadian network, CW4WAfghan, began. Today there are 13 chapters in Canada and an Afghan-run office in Kabul, all working towards advancing human rights for Afghan women.

In 1998, to learn more about the issues for Afghan women, Carolyn and Janice travelled to Toronto to meet author Deborah Ellis. Deborah had begun raising awareness about the plight of Afghan women in 1996 by forming a group called Women for Women in Afghanistan. When the women brainstormed about how to make this a national network, Deborah said, "I am not a fundraiser and I can't organize, but I CAN write!" After the meeting, she decided to go to meet Afghan women in refugee camps in Pakistan and Russia, to hear their stories directly and then share them with Canadians. Her work established one of the network's founding principles: listen to the voices of

Afghan women. Their experiences guide the network's actions. Deborah went on to write the award-winning young-adult novels of *The Breadwinner Trilogy* and *My Name is Parvana*.

By 1999 a Victoria, BC, chapter of the network was formed, followed by one in Oakville, Ontario. From these early beginnings CW4WAfghan members have remained focused on their goals of advancing rights and opportunities for Afghan women at a grassroots level, relying on a growing network of dedicated volunteers across Canada. Donations from individual Canadians are directed to programs – in health care, education, skills training and human rights awareness – run by or for Afghan women.

◇◇◇

I was very impressed. As I've noticed over the years of running and fundraising for Right To Play, the pieces always seem to come together at the right moment. It was very timely to hear from Leanne, as I had no time to lose in organizing what would be the Seventh Annual Run/Walk in Cochrane. This event had been going since the year I ran 250 marathons to raise money for Right To Play, and it had only gained momentum since then. This year, I wanted to shine a spotlight on the women and girls of Afghanistan.

In late November I received an email from Stephanie Case saying she wanted to Skype and discuss the year-end event. She told me that plans had changed. She couldn't get agreement from the parties involved for upgrading the volleyball court at Markaz High School and wanted to know if I would instead be interested in supporting another project for the girls. This would be a kayaking and camping trip for the women and girls in the Panjshir Valley in Panjshir Province in north-central Afghanistan. She said that the project would be totally in the control of Free to Run. I told her that the change in plan was no problem and that I would be happy to raise funds for this project.

And so, in early December, I met Leanne at a café in Calgary. I was thrilled that Canadian Women for Women in Afghanistan wanted to be involved. I explained to Leanne about the change in plans, and she was still on board. We spent an hour planning for the big day.

In the meantime, Kate and Scott were working on the film. In early December, the *Toronto Star* had printed an article about *The Secret Marathon* film, and in mid-December Kate received an email from the public affairs manager at the Embassy of Canada to the Islamic Republic of Afghanistan in Kabul, Greg Dempsey. Greg had read the article and was wondering if Kate wanted to do a joint event with Free to Run. His idea was to screen the completed film at the Canadian Embassy in Kabul. He also thought it might be interesting to co-host a panel discussion with some of the participants in the marathon. He signed off with enthusiasm: "Thanks and great work!"

This was excellent news, but the film screening was many months ahead of us. What I really needed to concentrate on was the Annual Run/Walk. I only had a week to finish all the planning.

The event, which was held at the Spray Lake Sawmills Family Sports Centre in Cochrane, went ahead without a hitch. Volunteers from the CW4WAfghan provided musical entertainment, set up a table of bags and scarves made by women in Afghanistan and provided information about the situation for girls in the country.

Despite the wintery weather, many people came out and gave their time, on New Year's Eve, to support the cause. Apart from the individual runners, there were lots of families and children. People covered distances varying from the full 42.2-km marathon to the popular 2K Cookie Run.

In total, we raised $7,000 for the Afghan girls to participate in kayaking and camping activities in the Panjshir Valley.

Kubra and I stayed in touch. She was very happy when I sent her and her brother, Amir, birthday cards and gifts in December. I told her about the fundraising event and how well it had gone. By this point, Kubra was working more and more with Free to Run, whose highlights for the past few years were very impressive.

◇◇◇◇◇◇ FREE TO RUN AFGHANISTAN HIGHLIGHTS, ◇◇◇◇◇◇
2014–2016

- Over 50 female students from our sports clubs in Afghanistan trained for and participated in a 10-km race outdoors in the Central Highlands region.
- Zainab, a Free to Run ambassador, became the first Afghan woman to run a full marathon in her country.
- Two ultramarathon teams from Afghanistan, including the first mixed-gender sports team from the country, successfully completed two 250-km self-supported footraces in the Gobi Desert and Sri Lanka.
- Twenty female students have gained access to weekly ski lessons, and five women competed in the 2016 Bamyan ski competition.
- Nelofar, a Free to Run ambassador and ultra athlete, started a running club of 20 women in northern Afghanistan and successfully organized a half-marathon for International Women's Day.

◇◇

Kate and I continued to communicate, talking about the film and our experiences in Bamyan, and about the messages we wanted to share about Afghanistan. In January I had some great news to convey to Kate. I had officially been picked to deliver a talk at TEDx YYC in June 2017, and I wanted to feature the Marathon of Afghanistan in my talk.

The journey towards TEDx started in August 2016 when I made my pitch to the TEDx YYC committee. This was a soul-searching exercise. The questions included: Why is your idea worth sharing? How does your idea relate to you personally? How do you know your idea works? And what is your call to action? I submitted my responses and waited.

In early January, I received a message from Kam Parel-Nuttall, a member of the TEDx YYC board, welcoming me officially to TEDx YYC 2017. I was over the moon, but I had no idea of the amount of work that lay ahead. All the while, a detail from my time in Afghanistan began to inch its way forward until it was something I could not ignore.

I recalled the day in Kabul when I had visited the British Cemetery and seen the plaques commemorating the fallen Canadian soldiers on the ground. I felt those fallen heroes should be shown more respect and wanted the plaques properly displayed.

So, I got in touch with Greg Dempsey at the Canadian Embassy in Kabul, the same fellow who was so supportive of the film. I figured he would know how to handle my request. I asked him if the plaques had since been installed and, if not, could he somehow see that this was done. It took some time and follow-up but, three months later, the plaques were installed. A small victory, to be sure, but a victory nonetheless.

Since returning from Afghanistan my running had been hindered by an issue with my right calf. I didn't think it was a serious injury, but it was very sore and so I decided to try and treat it with massage. I gave my old friend and chiropractor Greg Long (AKA Dr. Pain) a call. Greg had helped me in the past and was part of my medical support team when I ran my 250 marathons. Unfortunately, Greg was booked, but the receptionist suggested I see Greg's colleague, Nola, instead. So, I made an appointment for the following day.

Nola began by checking out my calf. She thought I had a problem with the fascia and told me she planned to do some "cupping" in the hope that it would relieve the pain and perhaps solve the problem. Now, this form of treatment was new to me. In fact, the only time I had ever heard of it was during the 2016 Summer Olympic Games, when television broadcasters showed the round bruises on Michael Phelps's back and said they were the result of cupping. I figured that if this centuries-old therapy worked for Phelps, it might work for me!

◇◇◇◇◇◇◇◇◇◇◇◇◇◇◇◇◇◇ CUPPING THERAPY ◇◇◇◇◇◇◇◇◇◇◇◇◇◇◇◇◇◇

Cupping therapy is a form of alternative medicine which applies localized suction to the skin. The therapist creates a vacuum in a glass cup that is then placed on the skin. The vacuum can be created either by heating and subsequently cooling the air in the cup or via a mechanical pump. Today, there are also silicone cups that can be pressed onto the skin. The cup is left in place for somewhere between five and 15 minutes. Therapists believe it helps treat pain, deep scar tissue in the muscles and connective tissue, muscle knots, and swelling.

Cupping has been practiced since 3000 BCE. Egyptian, Persian, and Saharan peoples have all employed cupping as a therapy in traditional practice. Hippocrates (400 BCE) also cupped patients to treat diseases and muscular issues. Muhammad is said to have highly recommended the therapy too, and it was practiced and developed by many Muslim health practitioners. Through these cultures, cupping entered Chinese and European societies. The earliest Chinese healer to practice cupping is recorded as Ge Hong, a Taoist alchemist/herbalist (281–341 CE).

<><><><><><><><><><><><><><><><><><><><><><><><><><><><><><><><><><><><>

Nola worked the cup up and down my calf, and it hurt. I have a very low pain threshold, and I freely admit that a couple of times I almost cried. By the end of the session, my calf was feeling very sore. I asked her if I could run the next day and she said to wait a couple of days before testing it out. I followed her advice and was amazed at the results. The soreness had gone away, and I had no problems during a 10-km run. I felt encouraged and ready to get back into training for my next event. Back in June 2016, I had signed up for the 2017 Calgary Marathon 150-km ultra, which was to be held to celebrate Canada's 150th birthday. The run was at the end of May, so I had four months to prepare. In late February, Sue and I took a trip to England. We flew into London and spent a couple of days with Calum in Wimbledon. Then he drove the three of us to Wales, where he had rented a cottage for four days. It was on a farm and, being lambing season, it was lovely to see the little lambs with their mothers in the fields among the wild daffodils.

At the end of the four days, Calum drove Sue and me to Bristol to pick up a rental car, and then he headed back to London.

Sue and I drove down to Newquay, in Cornwall, and the Rotary 1175 District Conference, where I'd been asked to give a keynote speech about my trip to Afghanistan. It gave me the opportunity to spread the word about the issues facing women and girls there and their desire for freedom and equality. I have been a member of Rotary in Canada for some years, and it was great to spend the weekend with some English counterparts. I also met up with an old friend, Stephen Lay, whom I have known since my days at mining college and who ran part of the South West Coastal Path with me in 2014. Sue's sister Lynne joined us at our hotel, for the weekend. Lynne has been a great supporter of all my fundraising initiatives, especially when I was running the South West Coastal Path, providing accommodation, transport and support for Sue.

From Cornwall we went to Devon for a visit with my sister Louise in Newton Abbot, and my youngest brother, Andy, joined us. I hadn't seen either of them in quite some time, and it was great to catch up and visit some of the old haunts from our childhood.

Finally, Sue and I headed to Dorset for a visit with our old friends Bob and Julie. They had been best friends with one of my sisters, Jan, who sadly passed away in 2011. Sue had known them for many years and worked with Julie at the local elementary school. In fact, it was in Bob and Julie's kitchen, back in 2003, that Sue and I first met.

Soon it was time to head back to Canada. The trip was the perfect intermission, the break I needed, before I continued with my work. The race wasn't over yet!

TWELVE

TEDX – LIFE IS A RELAY

"What you do makes a difference, and you have to decide what kind of a difference you want to make."

– JANE GOODALL,
British primatologist and UN messenger of peace

On March 13, I was saddened to hear that one of my running heroes, English-born Canadian Ed Whitlock, had passed away at the age of 86.

In 2004, at the age of 73, wearing a pair of 20-year-old running shoes, Ed ran the Scotiabank Toronto Waterfront Marathon in a world-record-breaking time of 2:54:49. Like me, he had come to running late in life when, in his 40s, he started running marathons with his son.

Ed ran to race, as they say, and couldn't think of a reason why someone his age shouldn't. As he wrote in *iRun* magazine:

When I raced in Rotterdam at age 74, some of the world's best marathon runners, Kenyans in their 20s and 30s, could not fathom why a person my age would be running a marathon and certainly not in that time. I did 2:58:40

that day and it blew their minds. This needs to change. Because if they can't imagine themselves doing the same thing, it will never happen. Why don't they think they can do the same thing?

When he was training, Ed liked to run in a local cemetery. "I like running in the cemetery," Whitlock once said. "Compared to everyone else there, no matter how you look when you're running, you look pretty good."

He was fast, but he was also modest. I'm going to miss seeing reports of his running. The last one I saw had been about his 3:56:38 finish at the 2016 Scotiabank Toronto Waterfront Marathon, just before I set out for Bamyan. It was another world record for his age. Few people, I discovered, had known about Ed's cancer diagnosis.

Ed's passing reminded me that time waits for no man. I knew it was time for me to get serious about training for the race I was planning to undertake at the end of May, the Confederation 150-km ultra in Calgary. It was a one-time-only event in celebration of Canada's 150th Anniversary, and I would be running and fundraising for Right To Play.

I had not been running as much as I should have been, because Sue and I had taken a trip to visit friends and family in the UK in February. And so, I planned a ten-week training schedule and on March 19 I set off for my first 30-km training run. At 6 a.m. I turned on my headlight, headed out from home and crossed the train tracks to Horse Creek Road. I could hear the coyotes howling in the foothills, so I picked up my pace. After 10 km I turned around. On my way back, a herd of deer crossed the road in front of me. I would see these creatures repeatedly as my ten-week training period progressed.

I arrived back at the house after completing 20 km. Time to change it up. The headlight went back into its bag, off came the woollen toque and heavy mitts. Time for a pair of light woollen gloves, and off came the jacket. I grabbed a cup of coffee and was soon on my way again. This time, I ran 5 km out and 5 km back. In total, 30 km. It was a good start to my training program.

At this point, I was still completing my tenure as writer-in-residence at the local library. I had been facilitating workshops and mentoring local writers in one-on-one sessions. One of the workshops I presented was Seven Steps to Getting Published. This addressed issues relating to blogging, self-publishing, book proposals, contracts, book launches – and the fact that after the book is published is when the real work begins. Then is the time to promote and market your book, and this can be an extremely time-consuming and frustrating process. I hope the participants took away some valuable advice and insights.

It was around this time that I read a report about a new project Free to Run had completed in Bamyan. They had received one-time funding from the Canadian Embassy in Afghanistan and the Conservation Organisation for Afghan Mountains (COAM) to construct an outdoor ice-skating rink. It was the first one in Afghanistan!

The project was aimed at girls and women in the region, aged ten to 25. Alongside the skating were lessons in greenhouse planting and composting. At first, I wondered, *Why skating and the environment?* Turns out the program was designed to reach a diverse group of girls who might be interested in sports *or* the environment, and have them experience both. Seventy girls and women attended in just one month.

The outdoor rink was built at a high altitude, so it lasted from January until March. The organization flew in an ice-skating coach, Britt Das, from Holland, so some participants could learn how to skate as they also undertook environmental training sessions. Participants from other regions were also flown in to take part in a special Winter Sports Week.

In the report, Taylor Smith noted that the skating seemed to break down barriers between the young women who were coming from different provinces. "At first, they were stuck with their little groups, like the Northern team, the Central team, etc. But once they were on the ice it took about five minutes for them to form new friendships. Mostly because they were helping one another to not fall over!"

Taylor also wrote: "Who knows – there could be some future Olympians in the program! There were a couple of little ten-year-olds who were phenomenal and became mini-teachers to the other girls. The younger girls picked up the sport very quickly and were doing spins and all sorts of things."

The beginnings of an idea were starting to form. I thought, *If they have a rink, that means they could play hockey!* I decided to contact Taylor with my idea: bring hockey to the girls and women in Bamyan.

At the beginning of May, I was feeling pretty good about myself and the progress I was making in my training. But then, on May 16, I felt a twinge in my right thigh. Experience has taught me that there are some things you can run off, others you must rest up and ice or heat, and others still for which you have to seek professional treatment.

Once again I found myself lying on the table in my chiropractor's treatment room having deep-tissue therapy and manipulation. This really helped, and after a few days of rest my thigh was feeling much better and I felt sure it would get me through to the race.

On Saturday, May 27, the big day arrived. The start line was at the Olympic Arch at Eau Claire Market in Calgary. I had arranged to meet a friend, Malc Kent, and prepare for the race. Some time back, I had met Malc through my local running club. He had joined us for our regular Saturday morning run. He explained that he was part of a start-up company that was developing technology able to monitor athletes' key running outputs like power, heart rate and efficiency of running motion. Malc told me he was interested in fitting me with data-collection modules to monitor my progress during races. So he put a pod on each foot, taped modules to my shins and fitted a data collector on my lower back. I hoped these items wouldn't weigh me down.

At 6 p.m., as it began to drizzle, the gun went off and so did I. As usual, my biggest nemesis was the cut-off time. I knew this one would be tough. The first 100 km had to be completed in 13 hours, and you had to get to the start line of the 50-km ultra by 7 a.m. The remaining 50 km had to be completed in 6.5 hours, a very big ask.

Things went well for the first six 10-km loops but, as darkness fell, I started to feel pressure. Running at night is very different from running during the day. The light plays tricks with my eyes and time seems to speed up. I kept going but, try as I might, when I hit the 95-km mark I knew I had run out of time. I was really disappointed I had not finished, but in the end, I was just happy to head home. The next day I looked up the results. Out of the 58 starters only 16 finished. These numbers really put the experience into perspective, and I didn't feel so bad about not finishing. Misery loves company!

At the same time, on the other side of Canada, another event was taking place, the Ottawa Marathon Weekend. Kate had entered the half-marathon, and at the end of her run she bumped into John Stanton, a runner, triathlete and writer of books on running and walking. John is probably best known as the founder of the Running Room organization. During the race, Kate had been wearing her Marathon of Afghanistan running shirt and John asked her about it. Kate told him about the trip to Afghanistan and running in the marathon there, supporting the girls and women struggling in their fight for the right to run. He was very interested in her story. After their conversation, she thought that perhaps John might consider being a corporate partner in the film. "I sent him an email," she told me. Little did either of us know, at that stage, where that initial conversation would lead.

Meanwhile, preparation for my TEDx YYC talk was in full swing.

Every speaker is allocated a speaking coach, and TEDx board member

Kam Parel-Nuttall was mine. From mid-January until late April, we worked on idea after idea and draft after draft. Concepts came and went, from "LSB (Long, Slow and Boring): A Brain Changer," to "Finish the Race Attitude," to "Life Is a Relay," which would be my chosen title and theme. By late April the outline for the talk was set, but then came the fine tuning. Every word had to count. In a 17-minute presentation, there is no room for padding or waffle. What I hadn't realized was that every word I was going to say had to be transcribed, and I wasn't allowed to waver from the script. This was very new for me. I always prepare for my talks, but I also have the advantage of being able to ad lib and make on-the-spot changes in response to audience reaction. With a TEDx talk, you can't do that. Hour after hour I would stand in front of a mirror or video camera, trying to deliver the talk exactly how I wanted it, bearing in mind that I couldn't change the wording. I did Skype rehearsals with Kam, and at times I wondered if, with all that rehearsing, the actual presentation would be wooden and emotionless. By mid-June I could recite the 2,119-word transcript in my sleep, and on Friday June 23, at 3:20 p.m., I gave my 16-minute, 15-second talk, "Life Is a Relay."

The preparation for the talk was incredibly rigorous, but like anything in life, you get out of it what you put in, and I hoped that all the hard work would pay off.

My experience at TEDx YYC lasted a day and a half. I arrived at 2 p.m. on June 22 at Calgary's Jack Singer Concert Hall with Gitti Sherzad, who would play an important part in my presentation.

I had heard about Gitti through Leanne Brintnell. A student at University of Calgary, Gitti had immigrated to Canada with her family when she was just a young girl. Now she is actively involved in fundraising for families in Afghanistan. I felt she would be perfect in helping me with my presentation, as I was looking for someone to whom I could pass the baton. I gave her a call and we arranged to meet at a Tim Hortons coffee shop, where I explained my idea. Luckily, Gitti was very excited at the prospect of being involved and agreed to appear with me on stage at the TEDx event.

The afternoon of June 22 was set aside for rehearsals, and over the next three hours we presenters practiced our talks in front of one another in small rooms located around the main stage. Kam, Gitti and I polished paragraphs and tweaked sentences. At 3:30, I got the call – it was time for my technical rehearsal. I walked onto the stage and looked out over the theatre. One of the technicians told me where the main camera was and told me to look in that direction. Then he pointed at a massive red dot and directed me to stand in the middle of it. Speakers, technicians and TEDx volunteers were milling around, trying to deal with last-minute issues.

I had little sleep that night, but, in the morning, I felt ready to attend a student breakfast at Hotel Arts in downtown Calgary. Students from Mount Royal University, the University of Calgary and Southern Alberta Institute of Technology (SAIT) arrived to talk with the TEDx presenters. The students had been selected for this experience, based on the strength of their compositions entitled "Why I Want to Go to TEDx YYC." I very much enjoyed chatting with the students. They were interested in discussing the topics of our talks, the TEDx process and what had made us get involved.

At 9:30 all the presenters were taken to the Jack Singer in Tesla electric cars. It was now a case of hurry up and wait. Once the talks were under way, I found a spot at the side of the stage where I could sit and watch the other speakers.

The speaker before me was Marni Panas. Marni is transgender and, in her talk entitled "Finding Courage, Conquering Fear," she advocated for diversity and inclusion. She is dedicated to creating safe, welcoming and inclusive environments, especially for the LGBTQ community. Her talk was very informative, passionate and inspirational.

Soon it was my turn.

Singer, songwriter and event presenter Michael Bernard Fitzgerald introduced me, and I walked onto the stage amid applause. The lights prevented me from seeing anyone other than those seated in the front row – the students I'd had breakfast with that morning. First things first, I walked to the centre of the massive red spot and looked at the main camera. So far so good. And then, I gave the following address, with accompanying slides.

I've often heard it said that "life is a marathon, not a sprint." However, having run a few marathons, I've come to believe that life is actually a relay.

I love watching the Olympics. One of my favourite events is the 4×100 relay race. The athletes line up, the gun goes off and they explode out of the blocks. Hitting their stride, they hurtle down the track with one objective in mind: to pass the baton to the next runner.

In life, exploding out of the blocks is that moment when you find your passion, the thing you were meant to do. Hitting your stride is the journey you take. You may not know the destination, but you're on the right path. Passing the baton is reaching out to someone and sharing your experiences.

Usain Bolt's reaction time at the start of a race is 0.155 seconds. However, it took me a lot longer to explode out of the blocks.

On December 9, 2001, my wife Wendy died of cancer. Over the following year I struggled with my grief and often felt empty and alone.

One evening, in December 2002, I got a call from my younger brother Peter. After some small talk, he got to the point: "I challenge you to a marathon," and with hesitation I said, "You're on!"

Now the only problem was, I didn't run. I was 47 years old and I had always had a bit of a rocky relationship with sport.

This is "baby" Martin, a child only a mother could love. Back then I was known as a "huggable" child. My size caused issues in school. When it came to sport in England, it was soccer, cricket and rugby, and I always got picked last for the team. I'm what you could call a "Reverse Olympian" – they're generally very good at one sport while I'm rubbish at lots of sports.

So, that same night Peter challenged me, I headed out. I was in my canvas tennis shoes, cotton jogging pants, fleecy top, woolly hat and big mitts. I ran 1 km out and 1 km back. Returning home, I was cold and wet and thought to myself, This is ridiculous, I've done 2 km and have another 40.2 to go. How on Earth could anyone run that distance? *However, I knew I couldn't back down from a challenge from my brother.*

I realized I needed help, so I joined the Sudbury Rocks running club. They taught me about nutrition, hydration, shoes and pacing. Over the next two months my mileage increased from 5 km to 10 km, and in April I ran the Ottawa half-marathon. Finally, it was July, and I was at the start line of the 2003 Calgary Marathon. Next to me was my brother Peter. And to show you how big a challenge this was, on the other side was my other younger brother Andrew, who had flown in from England.

This was Global Sibling Rivalry.

The gun went off and I flew from the start line. Then, at the 2-km mark disaster struck. I stepped in a pot hole and, smash, down I went. My knees were bleeding and my hands were all scraped up. Well, I brushed myself off and kept going. I finished the marathon in just under 4 hours. In the brotherly stakes, Andrew came first, I was second and Peter was third.

I felt elated to have completed the marathon. While dealing with my grief Peter had reached out to me and, in running, I had found my passion. Finally, I had exploded out of the blocks.

Usain Bolt's best relay split is 8.7 seconds, and he hits his stride in 60 m. In a 100-m relay, the path is very clear. You have a lane and you have to stay in it. However, in life the path is not quite so clear.

My running journey continued and took me to the 2004 Boston Marathon, but then in 2005 I signed up for a four-month cycling trip in Africa, from Cairo to Cape Town. Along the way, I played soccer and ping pong, and I ran with the kids. I realized the power of play and sport. It doesn't matter your age, gender, culture or religion: sport brings people together.

This experience stayed with me, but I didn't know what to do with it until one evening in February 2009 when a friend introduced me to Right To Play.

This organization uses sport and play-based programs to teach kids life skills such as leadership, team building and conflict resolution. That night, something clicked and I knew I wanted to help.

In mid-2009, I was training for my first 100-mile race, the Lost Souls Ultra, and while out on a five-hour run, I came up with the idea of Marathon Quest 250. This would involve attempting to run 250 marathons in one year to raise $250,000 for Right To Play.

So, on January 1, 2010, at 9 a.m., a group of us lined up on the 1A, outside of Cochrane. It was −32°C. The gun went off, and 5.5 hours later we were finished. One down, 249 to go.

During the year, my favourite days were Thursdays, when I'd run a marathon at one of the local schools.

I'd go in for morning assembly and talk to the kids about Right To Play. Then I'd go outside and run a hundred times around a school building or the soccer field. Around and around.

The kids would then come out and join me for the first couple of loops. Then they'd wave goodbye and head to classes. I'd keep going, and they'd wave to me from inside. At lunchtime they would come out for two more loops. As we ran, they'd feed me lunch. They'd give me apples, carrots and Snickers bars. I was like a running guinea pig, sort of a Pet for a Day.

Then they'd go in for afternoon classes. I'd keep going and at end of the day, after six hours of running, I'd be joined by the kids for the last two loops and we'd finish the marathon together and have high fives.

But what really blew me away was when they came up to me and gave me their pocket money for the "other" kids. They understood how lucky they were with their school, homes and toys, and then I shared with them that some children don't get the chance to play. These children might have to spend six hours a day fetching water from a tap in a village or they might live in refugee camps where it's too dangerous to go off and play.

I could have had the worst week of running marathons, but my spirits soared every Thursday after running at a school.

In total I ran at 60 schools with over 12,000 students from Kindergarten to Grade 12.

Marathon #250 was completed on December 31, and we had raised $320,000. I had found my path by using running to help underprivileged children, and I was hitting my stride.

Usain Bolt was a member of the gold medal-winning 2012 and 2016 Jamaican Olympic 4×100 men's relay team. One of the key factors for victory: successfully passing the baton.

In February 2015 I was hospitalized because of a massive blood clot on my brain. Suddenly, from running multiple marathons, I needed help to walk the 20 feet from the hospital bed to the bathroom.

My recovery was slow, and I was on a cocktail of drugs. But after two months I was allowed to go for short walks. In May I inched my way along to the finish line of the 2015 Calgary Marathon 5-km walk.

The months rolled by and one morning, in late October, my wife, Sue, showed me an article in the Guardian *newspaper. It was about the First Marathon of Afghanistan and a young woman named Zainab, who had become the first-ever Afghan woman to have run a marathon.*

What struck me were the challenges she faced in training. Normally, runners are dealing with issues of hydration, nutrition, blisters. For Zainab the issues were verbal and physical abuse. People would yell at her, "Get off the streets," and, "You're a prostitute," and they'd throw stones at her to stop her. She ended up training by running around and around inside her walled garden.

When I read this, I vowed that if I was ever able to run again, I would support the women in the Second Marathon of Afghanistan. At the end of May, I ran the 2016 Calgary Marathon, and at the end of October I was on a plane to Kabul.

When I arrived I met another marathon participant. Her name was Kubra, and she was being supported by Free to Run, an NGO working with girls and women in communities impacted by war and conflict. Unfortunately, her training had been interrupted by a bombing at her school, and she thought she would only be able to run the 10K. I asked if she would like to try and run the marathon together, with the aim of finishing within the cut-off time of seven hours. She said yes.

The race started at 8 a.m. on November 4 and was held in the town of Bamyan, 140 km northwest of Kabul. The course was brutal. It was an out and back and started at an elevation of 9,000 feet. The out section then had an elevation gain of another 1,200 feet. Kubra and I started a routine of running 9 minutes and walking 1. The key was to take hydration, nutrition and electrolytes at regular intervals. We reached the turnaround at 3 hours 36 minutes, and I knew that at this rate we wouldn't make the cut-off time. Also, Kubra was struggling. She was suffering from stomach cramps.

We continued with the 9s and 1s, but Kubra's cramps were getting worse and we started to walk. I knew Kubra was mentally tough and over the next two hours I used all my experience from 330 marathons to keep her going. I told her to take things in "ten-minute chunks," keep moving, and not to look beyond that. With 6 hours 45 minutes gone, we still had 1 km to go. We looked at each other and started running. We crossed the finish line at 6 hours 52 minutes. We had 8 minutes to spare.

I had gone to Afghanistan to support the women, and running with Kubra helped me do it. Kubra had already exploded from the blocks with her efforts to promote women's and girls' rights and was hitting her stride with the work she was doing with Free to Run. During the seven hours we were running, we worked together for a common goal. Kubra completed the marathon and the baton had been passed.

Now I'm at the end of this relay and it's time to hand off the baton. (I take a baton from my back pocket.)

I'd like to ask Gitti Sherzad to come up to the stage. (Gitti enters from stage left and joins me on the red spot.)

Gitti arrived in Calgary from Afghanistan at the age of seven with her parents and younger sister, Gee-Sue. She is studying at the University of Calgary, and Gitti and her team are presently organizing their first fundraiser to help victims of the devastation from the recent terrorist attacks in Kabul. These funds will go directly to the families most in need.

Gitti is doing something to make a difference. She's exploded out of the blocks and is starting to hit her stride.

Gitti, I'm handing over the baton to you. Take it and run with it. (I pass the baton to Gitti, we share a high five and she exits the stage.)

So, have you started your relay yet?

What will it take for you to explode out of the blocks?

Find your passion, and you're on your way.

Hitting your stride can be a long journey. The key is an openness to take a chance and a willingness to persevere. At the end of the relay, it's time to pass the baton.

So, reach out to someone, share your experiences, and make a difference in their life.

Thank you.

The high point for me was when Gitti joined me on stage and I passed the baton to her. As I left the stage, I thought, *It's done, and I got through it.* I felt it had gone well, and I was happy. I had spread my message about the importance of making a difference in people's lives and passing on passion and knowledge to others.

Life may be a relay but presenting a TEDx talk is definitely a marathon.

In 1984, Richard Saul Wurman and Harry Marks produced and presented the first TED (the convergence of technology, entertainment and design) which included a demo of the compact disc, the eBook and 3D graphics from Lucasfilm, while mathematician Benoit Mandelbrot demonstrated how to map coastlines using his theory of fractal geometry. Cool as the event sounds, it did not attract a big audience. In 1990, though, Wurman and Marks tried again with the TED Conference, which became an annual event of scientists, philosophers, musicians, business and religious leaders, philanthropists and other people sharing their knowledge and experiences. By 2001, the conference had gone non-profit, with Chris Anderson taking over as its curator.

Anderson's goal for TED was "inspired format, breadth of content and commitment to seek out the most interesting people on Earth and let them communicate their passion." In 2006, the first TED Talks to be posted online began to inspire and have an impact on millions of people, and it only grew from there.

The event I participated in was a TEDx, which was launched to support independent organizers who want to create TED-like events in their own communities.

◇◇

After the event, I met up with Sue and Gitti in the lobby, where we spent time mingling with the other speakers and audience members. I was delighted to hear several people tell me how much they had enjoyed my presentation and how the message of my talk had resonated with them. Some said it had inspired them to act and think of ways in which they could become involved in helping others.

Summer came to our little corner of Canada, and with it Canada's 150th birthday. On July 1, I decided to celebrate the freedom I have to run by fuelling a marathon with a Canadian classic: a Tim Hortons Dutchie.

This square, glazed, raisin-filled dream reminds me of the glazed dough-nuts I used to eat when my dad took me to car auctions in Exeter, Eng-land. I'd eaten them from the day I immigrated to Canada in 1977 un-til they were discontinued by Tim Hortons in 2014. I couldn't believe it when Sue brought a Dutchie home for me one day at the end of June. Tim Hortons had decided to bring them back for a limited time only. Sud-denly, the "Dutchie-fuelled" marathon began to take shape.

I wanted to find out how many Dutchies I would need to fuel a mara-thon, so I went to the Tim Hortons website to check out the delicacy's nu-tritional facts. One Dutchie contains: calories 240, sodium 200 mg, total fat 6 g (saturated 3 g), total carbs 40 g, fiber 1 g, sugar 17 g, protein 5 g, calcium 2%, and iron 15%. The numbers looked good. I figured that for a five-hour marathon I would need five Dutchies.

I set off at 6:30 a.m. on the cool but clear morning of July 1, Canada Day. My route was a 1-km loop around my house and along the Bow River. After 5 km I had my first half-Dutchie, microwaved for 10 seconds to give it that freshly baked taste. Around and around I went. My running buddy Wayne joined me, and he ran 16 km (1.5 Dutchies).

During the run, I kept up with social media, sharing such things as my favourite movie: *A Fist Full of Dutchies*; favourite book: *The Girl with the Dutchie Tattoo*; favourite song: *If I Had a Million Dutchies*; favourite quote: *Make the Dutchie great again*; favourite monument: *Stonehenge Dutchies*; and fa-vourite TV show: *Dutchie Is the New Black*.

At 4:49:16, the Tim Hortons Dutchie marathon was over.

Despite the joy of running on a Dutchie high, the marathon was not the highlight of the summer. No, that was reserved for when our 13-year-old granddaughter, Autumn, came to stay with us later in July. She came to us from the small town of Moose Creek, on the outskirts of Ottawa. We toured the mountains (she was impressed by Mt. Rundle, 2948 m), and we went to the Tsuut'ina Powwow and a variety of other special events in our neck of the woods. Her favourite outing was to the Yamnuska Wolfdog

Sanctuary, located on 160 acres of land about 20 km west of Cochrane. This is a place where this breed (domestic dogs crossed with wolves), often desired as puppies but then not properly understood and so abandoned, could find sanctuary and where people like us could go and find out more about them. Autumn loved seeing these wonderful creatures.

However, the highlight for me was when we ran 5 km together. This was her first 5-km run, and I must admit the route I picked was a little tough. She completed the distance in 43 minutes 48 seconds. I was really proud of her, and I was looking forward to the next time I might run with her.

THIRTEEN

CAMPING IN AFGHANISTAN, RACING IN CANADA

*"Afghan women often describe the difference
between men and women in just one word:
freedom. As in: Men have it, women don't."*

– JENNY NORDBERG,
author of *Underground Girls of Kabul*

From time to time in 2017, I would receive updates from Taylor and the work being done by Free to Run.

In mid-September I was excited to receive an email from her, updating me on the camping and kayaking trip the group took in August. It was amazing to hear about it, knowing that the funds raised on the run/ walk way back in December 2016 had helped make it a reality. Taylor wrote:

*This summer Free to Run embarked on an unprecedented camping and kayak-
ing expedition in the Panjshir Valley. Eleven girls and women from multiple*

provinces in Afghanistan participated. Not only was it their first experience in Panjshir Valley but it was the first time they had ever camped outdoors or kayaked. It was also the first time an Afghan female had ever kayaked in the country!

Upon arrival in Panjshir, the team visited the grave of Ahmad Shah Massoud, a famous Afghan political and military leader. The team then journeyed another two hours into the valley to set up a temporary camp at the base of one of the tallest mountains in the region. They had an introductory meeting over green tea and sweets with the district governor, police chief and elders, who were all interested in their experience as female adventurers. Although there were several concerns as to whether the team would be able to summit the mountain to attain the glacial lake at the peak, the participants managed to convince them of their capabilities with stories of running marathons and hiking through other Afghan mountains.

Twenty-one-year-old Hasina commented that the one new skill she learned on the trip was "camping. It changed my life. It showed that we can live without anything and just be happy!"

After well wishes, the team pulled all their gear and food from the van and set off on a one-hour hike up to a plateau camp for the night. Although only two participants were formally trained on setting up tents, the others took to it with enthusiasm. All their tents were set up before dark. After dinner, around a large campfire, the team turned in for the night. They were up again before dawn so they could get an early start and beat the summer heat. Although the climb was very steep, the girls remained in good spirits by playing music, singing and sharing stories about their home provinces.

They arrived at the lake, at an approximate altitude of 4425 m, five hours after departing from base camp, just in time to picnic on the shores for lunch. After a few hours of napping in the sun and exploring the lake, they started on the descent. After ten hours of hiking, the team started their second campfire to make dinner. They talked about the day and were very proud of what they had accomplished. Some of the village elders came to visit and were happily surprised to hear of their success. "*No women, not even most of the men in this village, are able to get up to the lake!*" they said.

Kayaking was next.

The original plan was to kayak the Panjshir River, but the authorities were worried about the girls' safety. These worries stemmed from the conservative culture of the valley. Free to Run found an alternative solution, which was to kayak on a lake outside Kabul. So the next day the team packed up camp to return to Kabul, where they would get their first lesson in kayaking on a lake on the outskirts of the city.

Before the participants could get into boats and start practicing strokes, the instructor, Joe, had to teach all but one of them how to swim. "They were exceptional in their attitude, confidence and willingness to try," he said.

A few hours later, the participants were gliding through the water in their own kayaks. Others practiced swimming nearby, waiting for their turn in the kayaks. Although Afghanistan is a dry, landlocked country, it is also home to many rivers and lakes traversing thousands of kilometres.

The girls and women were very thankful for the opportunity to participate in this groundbreaking trip. In the words of 21-year-old Fatima, who participated in the expedition: "Girls who do sports can be an example for others who live in narrow-minded places. We can encourage other girls to do sports on these trips."

Sue and I were both thrilled to hear about the success of the trip. It was good to know that the girls had been able to experience these activities and broaden their horizons.

I too had been keeping active, training for my final race of 2017 in late September. It was a big one: the Golden Ultra, a three-day, multi-stage race with a different event each day. I had been training throughout the summer by running the Fullerton Loop, just outside Bragg Creek, a 4-km route that climbs 305 m for 2 km before you hit the turnaround.

The Golden Ultra happens every fall, rewarding runners with stunning scenery and mountain views. It features three stages of running over three days. On the first day, the "Blood," a 5-km uphill run over dirt terrain, has 1000 m of elevation gain and kicks off at 4 p.m. The following morning at 7:30, the "Sweat" is a gruelling 60-km loop on single-track trails from the town of Golden to the summit of Kicking Horse Mountain Resort and back. Finally, at 9 a.m. on the final day, the "Tears" is a "flat, fast and funky" 20-km run over single-track trail through the woods. Participants can sign up to run one or more of the stages as individuals or they can complete the event in three-person relay teams.

◇◇◇

On the morning of September 22, I pulled into Golden, BC's municipal campground and found a place to set up my tent. The "Blood" portion of "Blood, Sweat and Tears," would take place that afternoon. I met up with some friends from Cochrane, Roy and Lana Ellis and their son Brett. We drove up to the Kicking Horse Resort and waited at the bottom of the gondola for the race to start.

At last the gun went off and we hurtled up the side of the ski hill. There were no breaks, and over the next 1:30:45 all I looked at were my shoes and the ground three feet in front of me. Reaching the top, I caught up with Roy, Brett and Lana, and we were all happy to take a ride down on the gondola.

Day two was the Sweat, 60 km of running mountains, including 2500 m of climbing. We started in downtown Golden and then headed west on the north and east sides of the Kicking Horse and Columbia Rivers. While the first 2 km were pretty flat, the next 32 km were much like speed mountaineering, the high point being at the top of the Kicking Horse gondola. Then it was down, down, down from there, back to downtown Golden.

My concern, with all my ultras these days, are the cut-off times. The

Sweat stage had a 12.5-hour limit, and with the terrain, I figured anything could happen. The Ellises and I arrived at the start line with 45 minutes to go. Also at the start line was my friend Malc Kent. He wanted to collect more data on my running and compare it to my efforts in the Calgary 150-km ultra.

The race started at 7:30 a.m., and the hours ticked slowly by. I tend to get in a zone when I run ultras, and I concentrate on continually monitoring my time versus distance covered. With 55 km completed, I was 10.5 hours into the race but I was fading fast. I slogged the last 5 km and came in at 11:52:12, with under 40 minutes to spare. I was just happy to finish, and Malc was pleased with the data collected.

That night I sat in the Ellises' warm trailer and reviewed what the race director had written about final stage, the Tears. It would begin downtown and then follow a flat trail along the Kicking Horse River for 2 km. Next, runners had to kick upwards for about 300 m of pain (perhaps tears), followed by another 1.5 km of rolling trail. We would then enter the Mountain Shadows trail system, trails with names including Selkirk Slacker and Huff and Puff, Magic Dragon, and Trial and Error. The director said it was easy to navigate all these trails by just "staying right."

The next morning, Malc strapped me up again, and at 8 a.m. the gun went off. The cut-off time for this final stage was five hours and, the way I was feeling, I thought I would need every minute of it. My legs were killing me, and I had a large blister on my right foot from the Sweat. However, things soon started to turn around.

My favourite type of running trail is in woods on pine needles. It turned out that this route just flowed along for me at a slight decline and even the ups were short and sharp. I found I could power through them. I started to get into a groove. My legs began to feel better and the blister didn't cause me any problems because of the nature of the footing. I was finally loving the event! Before I knew it, I had finished the half-marathon in 2:56:29, well within the five-hour limit.

In early October, I again heard from Taylor at Free to Run. She had been run off her feet, preparing for the next Marathon of Afghanistan. She had thought about my ice hockey idea, but she felt the girls might not be ready to play hockey – not for another year. She wrote, "Since last year was the first year building the ice rink and the first time any of them had ever been on skates, we have a few kinks to still work out. I still cringe every time I think about the process of getting our skates in last year...took five months and the Ambassador of Afghanistan to the United States had to get involved before they released them to us!"

I was a bit disappointed but understood where she was coming from. But then she went on to ask if I'd be interested in helping fundraise to get their ice rink up and operational again for the coming winter. "Is this something you'd be interested in for your Eighth Annual Run/Walk fundraiser? The girls could really benefit from a full season of ice-skating practice this year."

I said yes and was excited to be fundraising for Free to Run again.

While the new fundraising goal put some spring in my step, for a while I hadn't been happy with my running and I felt I needed something to re-ignite my passion. I checked back on all my races and noticed that I had set all my personal best times in the 5-km, 10-km, half-marathon and marathon in 2003, at the age of 47, some 15 years ago. An idea came to me that maybe I could try and beat those times in 2018, at the age of 62. I knew that to at least attempt to achieve this goal I needed help, and I knew who to call on.

The next day I contacted Malc Kent and asked if he would coach me. Malc had been working with a couple of local runners and getting excellent results. We met at his house, and after a short chat we shook hands and came up with a title for my challenge: 62 Beats 47.

Malc set up a training program, and we started meeting every Wednesday morning to review my progress. The times I was shooting for were a huge stretch. In the 5K, 21:05; the 10K, 42 minutes; the half-marathon, 1:30:01; and the marathon, 3:22:44. Each week Malc set me up with an easy run, a long run, and a specific session such as tempo, intervals or hills.

We identified several races I should enter in 2018, starting with a 5K in Airdrie in mid-April and finishing with the California International Marathon in Sacramento on December 2. I felt revitalized, knowing I had a plan. My passion had returned.

On October 27, 2017, the third annual Marathon of Afghanistan was held. It was funny to think it was only a year ago that I was there, running with Kubra, taking in that breathtaking Bamyan landscape, eating at *chaikhanas*, listening to the words of Kausar as he explained the history of that amazing place. This time, 12 girls and women, supported by Free to Run, participated and they all finished. Kubra was one of them. I was thrilled that she had finished, despite not achieving her goal of being First Lady. I knew she'd been training hard while working for Free to Run. I followed the social media feed and watched a report on the event by NBC News.

◇◇◇◇◇◇ RUNNING WITH FARAHNAZ AND ZAHRA, ◇◇◇◇◇◇ FREE TO RUN'S NEWEST AMBASSADORS

On a cold dark September morning, Free to Run's two newest Ambassadors, Farahnaz and Zahra, competed in an ultramarathon with the Berkshire Ultra Running Community for Service (BURCS) in the hills of Massachusetts. The 50-mile race was tough, but for these two young women from Afghanistan, it was a race they were determined to finish.

Farahnaz and Zahra met at a boarding school in Kabul in 2010 and have been studying on competitive scholarships in the United States while simultaneously taking up running. Both started their running adventures with a half-marathon in 2015, followed by several full marathons. Step by step, they gained the confidence and experience needed to tackle the 50-mile ultra hosted by BURCS.

The BURCS community has been an early and dedicated supporter of Free to Run. The group was founded in 2013 by three passionate long-distance runners from western Massachusetts who felt they could combine running with social, civic and environmental issues. This race is called The Free to Run Race. BURCS's pillars of Run, Give, Inspire and Achieve fit perfectly with Free to Run's ethos of empowerment through sport.

Before starting the race, Farahnaz and Zahra had the opportunity to speak with their fellow runners about what it meant to be female runners from Afghanistan. Farahnaz shared that as a child, she wanted to be a boy because the boys were allowed to do all sorts of sports and activities that girls were simply not allowed to do. She used to wish for rainbows because in Afghan legend it's said that if you walk under a rainbow you can change your gender. As a ten-year-old child running in sandals, Zahra placed first in a local race and won a bicycle. Out of fear for her safety, her family said she would not be allowed to ride the bicycle. Both young women had overcome much just to be at the race.

The race course was mentally and physically challenging. The first loop had been fun but, by the second loop, Zahra's feet felt like they were on fire. At times she cried with frustration and pain from all the blisters on her feet. There was no doubt in Zahra's mind that this was the hardest thing she had ever done. She was truly pushed to the limit when she hit her foot on a rock before heading into the fourth and final loop. Thanks to the amazing support from course director Jake Dissinger, some dedicated pacers along the route, and Zahra's sheer determination, she managed to finish the race in 16 hours. No doubt the best moment for Zahra came at the end of the 50 miles, when she ran in to the arms of her coach who was waiting for her at the finish line.

Farahnaz had a very impressive race, finishing third female and eighth overall. The success of her day was tinged with tragedy as she had lost her beloved brother the week before the race. Her training had been thrown off course, but she knew that giving up was not an option. She had come this far, and she knew her brother would have wanted her to compete. Her family and friends advised her to "Wrap your brother in your heart and just run with him."

Zahra and Farahnaz are working to change the narrative of Muslim runners in the West.

◇◇

FOURTEEN

ICE-SKATING IN AFGHANISTAN

*"If I can skate on a thin blade
across ice, I can do anything."*

– KUBRA JAFARI,
Afghan program officer for Free to Run

In mid-November, Sue and I went to an event where Hayley Wicken-heiser was the keynote speaker. Hayley is a former Canadian women's ice hockey player. She is a four-time Olympic gold-medal winner and the first woman to play full-time professional hockey in a position other than goalie. I had met Hayley a few times, as she, like me, is an athlete ambassador for Right To Play. I had seen her most recently when we were both giving talks at TEDx YYC. At the end of that November evening, I had a chance to chat with her. She explained that she was right in the middle of preparing for the 2017 edition of Wickfest, her annual World Female Hockey Festival, where women's and girls' teams from all over the world get together for a tournament. This year a team from China was participating.

I told Hayley about my year-end fundraiser for the ice rink in Bamyan,

Afghanistan. Like me, she thought it would be great to get the girls playing hockey. I explained that it probably wouldn't be this year, but who knows what might happen in the future? Hayley agreed and said she was hoping Wickfest 2018 would host a team from India. From little acorns grow mighty oaks.

In early December, Sue and I went to see *The Breadwinner*, an animated feature based on Deborah Ellis's book. It was only shown in one cinema, the Cineplex Sunridge Spectrum in Calgary, and only for a week, but over the next three months it got some terrific reviews.

◇◇◇◇◇◇◇◇◇◇◇◇◇◇◇◇◇ *THE BREADWINNER* ◇◇◇◇◇◇◇◇◇◇◇◇◇◇◇◇◇

BOOK AND ANIMATED FEATURE

Deborah Ellis, a member of the Toronto chapter of CW4WAfghan, wrote *The Breadwinner* trilogy and *My Name is Parvana*. These award-winning books tell the story of Parvana and her close friend Shauzia, who lived in Taliban-controlled Afghanistan. Parvana dresses as a boy and works in the streets of Kabul to feed her family. Together, she and Shauzia dream of a peaceful Afghanistan.

The book was taken on by Canadian and Irish producers and adapted as an animated feature film. Angelina Jolie became an executive producer. Jolie has had her own experiences in Afghanistan, where she has funded two primary schools for girls. At the Toronto International Film Festival, Jolie said, "I really love this story because it's so much about family." Jolie hit the nail on the head when she commented that the story is "so powerful because it rings true for the situation of families wherever there is conflict or poverty or adversity."

◇◇

Sue and I hoped that *The Breadwinner* film would reach millions, encourage people to read Deborah's book and inspire them to act to help others. We were getting ready for the run/walk fundraiser at the time. I kept thinking about all the efforts that had been made at the beginning of 2017 to introduce the Afghan girls and women to ice-skating. And I was thrilled that Free to Run had come up with a fundraising idea for my Eighth Annual Run/Walk, to reinstall the ice rink and hold a Winter Sports Week for Afghan girls and women from the town of Bamyan and other provinces in Afghanistan. I really wanted the event to raise $5,000 for the skating rink.

As usual, December 31 would be the day for the Annual Run/Walk. In its almost eight years, this event had never been cancelled, but the weather the week leading up to it this year had been brutal. The forecast for that day was −32°C.

The day before the event, I asked Paddy, the operations manager at Spray Lake Sawmills Family Sport Centre, if he had any thoughts for a backup plan. He kindly offered to let people use the indoor track, free of charge, if the weather was simply too grim.

So, I sent out emails and posted updates, letting as many people as possible know that it was still a go. I had my fingers crossed that the weather would break and warm up. No such luck. On the morning of the event, I was up at 5:30. I checked the temperature. It was −48°C with the wind chill. Not good, but I was still thinking the outdoor route might be possible.

Upon reaching the centre, my first task was to mark the route by spray-painting orange arrows. Every 30 seconds the nozzle on the spray can froze and I had to keep going back to the car to thaw it out. At one point, I was driving along the side of the path and spraying the arrows from inside the car.

Soon, 9 a.m. came around, and a hardy group lined up at the start, outside the main entrance. I blew my whistle and away we went. My friends Hiro and Angie came down from Edmonton. They have participated every year in the fundraiser, and Hiro had completed 50 km in the bitterly cold weather by the end of the day. The route took us around the building, through Bow RiversEdge Campground, along the Bow River pathway and down to the turnaround spot at an old bridge. One loop is about 2.5 km, and in the first hour I managed to cover four. By this time, my hat and facemask were caked with ice and snow. After a short break, I headed out again and was joined by a few more runners and walkers.

Leanne Brintnell was there, organizing the band HYMN, a traditional fusion music band that focuses on traditional melodies from all around the world. They entertained everyone with some beautiful traditional music. Leanne, her daughter Erin, and Gitti also sold products made by women in Afghanistan, including purses, bags and scarves.

Our son Calum was over, too, visiting from England. He and Sue ran the registration desk.

The day went on, with runners coming and going. Everyone was doing their part and, by making donations, they were making a difference. At 2:40 p.m. it was time to do the final 2-km Cookie Loop. A bunch of kids lined up and I blew the final whistle. Twenty minutes later it was done. The kids got their medals and cookies, we packed up and everyone headed home.

I was really looking forward to a soak in the hot tub and a glass of Guinness, not to mention celebrating New Year's Eve with Sue and Calum.

FIFTEEN

THE SECRET MARATHON 3K

"I attribute my success to this —
I never gave or took an excuse."

– FLORENCE NIGHTINGALE,
English nurse and social reformer

T he *Globe and Mail* website reported that on December 31 the king penguins at the Calgary Zoo were brought inside due to the extreme cold. The next day, the *Calgary Herald* reported: "Cochrane Runners Go Where Penguins Fear to Tread."

The fundraising event had seen 65 participants, 30 of whom were brave enough to run/walk outside. We raised an amazing $2,936 on the day, but we still had a way to go to reach the $5,000 I wanted to send to Free to Run. Fortunately, during the following three weeks, cheques came in from the Cochrane Footstock weekend, the Cochrane Red Rock Running Club, and Rotary District 5630. By January 19 we had raised $6,031.

The day after we surpassed our fundraising goal was an early start. I felt energized by our success, and I was looking forward to leading the Rotary Raucous Relics, a team made up of members from the local Rotary club, to success in the Kimmett Pond Hockey Tournament, a fundraising event I'd taken part in for a few years. The tournament honours Lindsay

Kimmett, an athlete and aspiring doctor who passed away tragically in 2008 at the age of 26. Funds raised go to a foundation that invests in the community in Lindsay's name.

My team was scheduled for three games, the first of which was at 8 a.m. on the outdoor Mitford Pond. This was my fourth year playing for the Rotary team at this event and it had always been a great day. The game started on time, and I was on the first line. The ice was a little rough, with a few significant cracks. I felt good and made a couple of moves in the first minute, but then I made one move too many. My right skate got caught in a crack and I started to fall backwards. The skate didn't come out of the crack as I fell, and I could feel something give in my ankle. What a mess. The other players gathered around me and helped me off the ice.

I hobbled back to the car. Fortunately, I was still able to drive, so I headed home. Sue was surprised to see me, and I had to tell her the whole sad story. I quickly placed an old faithful on my ankle, a packet of frozen peas, and wrapped it up tight. My hockey tournament was over.

On the last day of January, I went to see Coach Malc, and he was not impressed. He tested my ankle as I walked on the treadmill and told me that for the next while I would be using our elliptical. He also prescribed his Four Pillars of Recovery: elliptical, ice on injured area, swimming, and warm-water therapy. It seemed like this might be a long haul.

I knew I still had to dive into my projects for the beginning of 2018: 62 Beats 47, and another project that I was incredibly excited about, The Secret Marathon 3K.

In contrast to my start on 62 Beats 47, The Secret Marathon 3K plans were going well. After the initial meeting with John Stanton, at the 2017 Ottawa marathon, Kate had shared her idea to have an event in conjunction with the Running Room and Canadian Women for Women in Afghanistan. Ideas went back and forth, and the outcome was that Running Rooms across the country would host 3K runs to fundraise for *The Secret Marathon* film. A team was set up that included John, Running

Room national events director Liz Caine, Leanne, Kate and me. We picked Wednesday, March 7, as the date for the event, which tied in with the weekly Run Clinics held at 6:30 p.m. at all Running Room stores, as well as with International Women's Week. Canadian Women for Women in Afghanistan had also come on board, which determined which cities would host the events, as the organization had volunteered its members to act as race directors in the ten cities that had branches. Kate wrote an article for the Running Room magazine that spelled out the thinking behind the event.

I ran my first marathon in Afghanistan, but that wasn't where I felt the most scared while running, it was in Canada. No one should have to feel scared when they run, so we're launching a race to celebrate everyone's right to be free to run, and we need your help to make it happen.

The day I felt scared running was one of those days when everything takes longer than you expect, and my run got pushed back later and later in the day until I was finally lacing up my shoes long after the sun had already set. I sent a quick text letting my husband know where I was running, and set off into the dark. Any time I run at night I have my senses on full alert and this was no different, searching around every corner for possible cars that might fail to see me, looking for wildlife but mostly being very much aware of what I can't see and what might wait for me in the shadows. I rounded a corner and there was a large group of men laughing loudly, clearly drunk. One smashed a bottle on the ground, another catcalled me and a third yelled out an inappropriate comment. I picked up my pace, my heart pounding. I pulled out my phone, called a friend and asked her to stay on the line until I knew I was out of range of the men. I was scared.

The freedom to run outside and run free says a lot about a place. Where we see people able to run, we know it is likely a country free of war. It means the people there are prosperous enough to choose to be active rather than it being necessary for survival. I've often taken it for granted that I can lace up my shoes and go for a run in Canada without having to think about whether or not I will step on a landmine or whether I will be threatened by terrorists, but this isn't the case everywhere.

A year and a half ago, I was invited to Afghanistan to create a documentary film called The Secret Marathon, about a community fighting for the right to be free to run. They organized the first-ever Marathon of Afghanistan as a mixed-gender race. The women who wanted to participate faced rocks being thrown at them, being insulted and having terrorists threaten them when they trained in the streets. But they persevered, running laps in their enclosed court-yards to train for the marathon so they could make a stand for equality. This community, in Bamyan, Afghanistan, has discovered something: if you can create a safe race you can help to create a safe place.

As my team and I worked on the film and met the community behind the Marathon of Afghanistan we learned that to create a place where everyone is free to run, it takes three key things: collaboration, courage and a bold vision. The Marathon of Afghanistan brings men and women together, racing alongside one another in a symbol of equality. They are allies. The Marathon of Afghanistan requires collaboration between runners from across the country, charities such as Free to Run, and businesses, including Untamed Borders. It takes a community that is willing to have courage in the face of difficulty. But most of all it takes a bold vision to create the first marathon in a country where running is not the norm, all in an effort to change the perception of Afghanistan and help the world see a different vision. A vision of a country where courage, equality and community are celebrated.

Coming back to Canada after witnessing this amazing event, I wondered if we could adopt these same strategies to make sure everyone in Canada felt safe to run outside. As my friend Val suggested, what if safe races could make safe places? We have also set a bold vision. We are inviting people in 10 cities across Canada to join us and be part of our community of allies who will celebrate the right of every person to be free to run. Our film, The Secret Marathon, *is collaborating with the Running Room and the charity Canadian Women for Women in Afghanistan to host the first-ever The Secret Marathon 3K. We want you to join us in this movement of equality.*

On the eve of International Women's Day, March 7, 2018, we are asking you to join us as we head out into the dark together to reclaim our communities and stand in solidarity across our country in the belief that everyone should be free to run.

The race directors included Jill in Victoria, Friba in Vancouver, Cheri in Kelowna, Lana in Edmonton, Leanne in Calgary, Mariam in Winnipeg, Kate in Toronto, Daphne and Melodie in Peterborough, Marg in Kingston and Jennifer in Ottawa. I was acting as the overall race director, and every Thursday at 5 p.m. MST we would all have a Skype call to see how things were going. The event would be hosted by a Running Room store in each of the designated cities, and the race directors, working with the Running Room events manager, had many elements to pull together.

The directors were getting permits for their routes, finding volunteers to operate the registration tables, route marking and patrolling the course, finding race officials, promoting the event in their cities, contacting media, sending out press releases, and making sure they had refreshments for the participants and volunteers. Many of the directors had not taken on anything like this before and, at times, they were overwhelmed. However, they were all enthusiastic and determined to ensure that the event went well.

During each Skype call I would tell everyone how many participants had signed up. By February 1 we were sitting at 135. But soon something strange happened. We started getting requests from people outside the ten cities who wanted to be part of The Secret Marathon 3K. We knew we couldn't set up official races everywhere, so we decided to offer a "Virtual Location" registration option, so anyone could sign up and do the 3K wherever they lived.

This new option gave me an idea. I had lived in Sudbury, Ontario, for 18 years, and the city had a Running Room store. I was sure I could get some family, friends and fellow runners from the city interested in doing the 3K, but I needed a race director. My thoughts turned immediately to my 14-year-old granddaughter, Autumn. I had recently noticed that her Facebook posts included some runs she had completed, and she sure seemed to have enjoyed them.

I gave her a call, and, after some small talk, I asked her if she would like to be the race director for The Secret Marathon 3K in Sudbury. I explained what it was and she excitedly said yes. I then talked to her dad, Ross, and he was fully in support.

When I shared this information with the other race directors, some were surprised. "Martin, isn't she too young to take this on?" I truly believe that young people between the ages of eight and 18 are capable of far more than we think. The issue is that we, as adults, do not give them the opportunities to take steps into the unknown. Of course we need to be there to guide and mentor, but we don't always need to hold their hands. Besides, she not only had her dad's support, but I had put her in touch with my friend Vince Perdue from the Sudbury Rocks Running group, and I had regular chats with her about how things were going and what she needed to do. I had become a kind of mentor in this situation. It is always good to pass on your experience and enthusiasm to a younger person, as well as offering ongoing encouragement, just as I had with Kubra, during our marathon experience.

◇◇◇◇◇◇◇◇◇◇◇◇◇◇◇ AFGHANISTAN'S FIRST ◇◇◇◇◇◇◇◇◇◇◇◇◇◇◇ MIXED-GENDER RUNNING TEAM

In 2017 Free to Run opened its program in Kabul to Afghan men, inviting them to join in the sports, learning and volunteering activities alongside Afghan women. This followed the success of the Free to Run mixed-gender ultra-marathon team, which competed in a 250-km self-supported footrace in Sri

Lanka in February 2016. Men and women training, learning and competing together side-by-side may not seem revolutionary, but in Afghanistan it was actually unprecedented. At this writing, the team remains the only mixed-gender sports team in the entire country.

◇◇◇

Kubra is now a program officer at Free to Run, and she is part of this team. In February 2018, she looked back on the team's history.

I remember the first day of our running training. We arrived at the training location very late. Picking up the team and organizing everyone took so long! We have to pick up all of the team members for safety — we keep our training locations secret, so they don't even know where they are going. We just did 15 minutes of running. It was short but enjoyable, as I was running freely in a secure place alongside my new teammates.

A year has passed since that day, but I still remember it well. Our team became the first mixed-gender team in the country. We had females and males running alongside one another. In Afghanistan. It was very difficult at the beginning.

Some challenges were normal, especially making everyone get up very early in the morning (3:30 a.m.) to run. Sometimes, they did not want to run and felt like just walking, so I'd jump in and do my best to motivate them to be ready for the marathon.

Sometimes, the challenges felt like they were more related to gender. Some of the boys would argue with me over my decisions as the program officer. A few of them left the team because of this, which made me sad. I would like to help them come back to the team if it were possible to solve the issues, but if not, I wish them a happy life.

As the year continued, new people joined the team. This time I got more energy to go forward strongly and help them to explore new things, such as running in a new place.

Sometimes, I had to struggle with guards, police and people in the community in order to let us run. We had permission letters from the authorities to be able to run, but people were not always comfortable with females and males running together. I remember once I had a fierce argument with two policemen who assumed we were "bad" women and men because we were training alongside one another.

Despite these challenges, I love my team and they are my family now. I feel their pain, and their happiness makes me happy. I enjoy every moment being with my team, and I love the sounds of group laughter when we are together and those crazy photo-shoot times.

When they crossed the finish line in the 3rd Marathon of Afghanistan in 2017, that was the best reward they gave me. I hugged them, looked at them, and told myself that was it: these individuals did their first marathon and showed to the world that they are strong enough to go forward together and run more freely.

Running changed me and showed me my strengths. I can see these changes in my team. Now they are ready to lead their own teams, fight for their rights, and help others around them through volunteer work. I see more than athletes; I see future leaders.

It was great working with Autumn on a project. Whenever I'd email her, I'd title the message "To: Race Director Autumn." She was making posters and putting them up in locations around Sudbury. Vince and the Sudbury Running Room manager, Eric, were giving her lots of support, and one evening she made a presentation to a group of runners at a Wednesday-night clinic.

By February 22 the number of people registered for The Secret Marathon 3K had reached 281. I must admit, with only 13 days to go, I thought the number might have been a little higher. The target was 500 participants from across Canada, so we still had some work to do. Everyone was working hard, and all we could do was push forward. One piece of good news was that Viiz Communications had agreed to be the national sponsor for the event's wristbands. Other good news was that we had our first international registrations from the USA and UK, and the donations for CW4WAfghan had reached $2,370.

During one of our final meetings, the question of race bibs came up. I suggested a unique possibility for the design. The bibs would not have race numbers but the word "EQUALITY." This way participants could print a bib off from wherever they were, whenever they wanted.

What a difference a week can make. On March 1 we had 425 registrants, and on March 2 we hit our 500-participant target. Radio, newspaper and TV media had started to pick up the story, and our numbers were jumping up each day. I was contacted by Meredith McMorran, a teacher at École Notre-Dame des Vallées, a local school in Cochrane. They wanted to do their own Secret Marathon 3K on March 7 at 3:30 p.m. Meredith wondered if I would come out and run with them. "Of course!"

On February 27 I had sent Zainab an email letting her know about The Secret Marathon 3K. I told her about the virtual location option and wondered if she and her colleagues might want to sign up. I didn't hear back from her until March 4, only three days before the event. Her message brought tears to my eyes.

Hi Martin,

I have discussed with my friends and colleagues; 15 persons are ready to participate in this race. We would involve the security and the mayor of the area that we would run in, Airport Street in Mazar-e-Sharif. Today I am going to talk with the responsible persons for security in person, after your confirmation. I have 2 questions for you:

1. Is there any certificate that you could send me the soft template of that we could give at the end of the race to participants?

2. As participants are students and they don't have any income, is it possible for them not to pay a fee for registration? Instead they will pay $1 each for transportation, refreshments and printing costs, as well the cost for the cars that will escort us during the race.

We all will be so excited to do it!

With regards,

Zainab

⸻

It was Zainab who had inspired me when she ran the First Marathon of Afghanistan, and now she was leading a group of friends to run in our The Secret Marathon 3K.

Later that day, I heard from Taylor, who wrote to let me know how the Bamyan Winter Sports Week had turned out. I knew they had gone ahead and reinstalled the ice rink and had been offering winter sports programming, but I hadn't yet seen anything mentioning ice-skating. In addition to some ski programming and bicycle training, the Winter Sports Week included ice-skating training for two people (a young man and a young woman from Bamyan), a program called Introduction to Hockey Basics and Puck Handling on Ice, as well as the first Band-e Amir Ice-Skating Challenge (with 12 female and eight male participants).

Taylor wrote, "Although we weren't able to get up to the skill level to play ice hockey, we were able to teach a lot of the basics through street-hockey sessions. Given how much the girls LOVED the game, I'm confident they'll be able to play on the ice next year. We also now have eight hockey sticks to practice with in the spring/summer!"

Apparently, the coach Free to Run hired to teach the girls ice-skating had also coached hockey for several years. Taylor seemed excited about the rink and was thrilled to see the growth in skills and support from the local community. "We've now got two Afghans comfortable enough on skates to lead their own lessons, which I know will make a world of difference next year!"

For my part, I couldn't believe it. The girls had tried their hand at hockey! I made a note to myself to let Hayley Wickenheiser know. Who knows? Maybe her Wickfest could host an Afghan team sometime in the future.

After hearing all this amazing news, I was thinking we had the 3K event well in hand. I didn't think there would be a problem in taking a bit of a break, so Sue and I sat down to watch the Oscars. We had already selected who we thought should win in the various categories. After watching *The Breadwinner* in December, Sue and I were most interested in the Best Animated Feature category. We wanted to cheer the film on to a win!

When it finally came time to announce the Best Animated Feature, the Oscar went to *Coco*. Sue and I consoled ourselves, knowing that its very nomination would increase *The Breadwinner*'s viewings by thousands. Many people who had never heard of *The Breadwinner* had heard of it now.

When Monday dawned, the final push was on for The Secret Marathon 3K. I checked our numbers; we were at 567 registrants. By the morning of March 7, race day, we had hit 724.

At 8:30 a.m., Liz, Leanne, Kate and I had a final conference call. Everything was in place and we wished each other all the best. Liz made a prediction that we would end up with over a thousand participants.

At noon I sent out a final list of participants, by city, to the race directors. As I put the list together, I noticed a very interesting statistic: the gender split was 78 per cent women and 22 per cent men. This is a trend that is being seen in races everywhere on Earth, a trend that bodes well, I think, for women participating in sport all over the world.

At 1 p.m. I gave Autumn a call. She said she was excited and nervous. I told her she had done all she could do by this point, and now she just had to enjoy the event. I knew her dad, Ross, would be with her every step of the way, so she was in good hands. At 3:30 p.m. I headed 1 km down the road to École Notre-Dame des Vallées. A group of 15 students, teachers and parents was lined up wearing EQUALITY bibs. I did a countdown, blew the whistle and off we went, across the road and onto the Bow River pathway. It was a beautiful day and everyone ran or walked the 3K at their own pace. At the end, it was high fives all around. I wanted to stay and celebrate with the group, but I had no time to spare, as I had to be at the Calgary event by 5 p.m. I picked up Sue and our friend Cathy, and we made a beeline to the city, where we met up with Cathy's husband, Wayne.

At Eau Claire Market, Leanne and her team of volunteers were busy getting ready. With 15 minutes to go, the open area was packed, and John Wilson from Viiz Communications said a few words of support and encouragement. Then Leanne and I joined him on stage, and the count-down started.

It was such a beautiful clear night that Sue, Cathy, Wayne and I decided to walk. The route was an out and back, so we had the opportunity to chat with people along the way. It was great to hear why they had decided to come along and support the event and donate to our project. My race time for the 3K was 36:27, a personal best (first time for that distance). Back at the market everyone was sharing stories and enjoying live music. What an incredible night. Everyone involved said how much they had enjoyed it and asked if we would do it again next year. Sue and I headed home and were thrilled with how everything had turned out. There had been over 250 runners and walkers at the Calgary event.

The next morning the final numbers were in. There had been a surge of walk-in participants just before the event, and this led to a final figure of 1,113. Liz had been correct. The donation for CW4WAfghan was $7,210.

I phoned Kate to see how things had gone in Toronto. She told me that they had had 165 participants at the event. A group of eight- and nine-year-old students from Chester Elementary School's running club participated and were the first to sprint across the finish line. One woman told her that this was the first time she had ever run a 3K. She was so excited and proud to meet her personal goal. The first young woman to register on the day of the event heard about the 3K for the first time that morning reading *Metro News*. And MP Nathaniel Erskine-Smith was so impressed with the event that he said if we would ever like him to do more than just show up to do the countdown, he would be happy to help.

KATE'S JOURNEY: AFTER THE MARATHON

Films are their own type of marathon. We decided to call ours The Secret Marathon.

So, what stays with me from the journey so far? The knowledge that I am not alone, the power of taking one more step, and the belief that if we continue to have faith, this story will be told. There was always a 50 per cent chance of failure for this project. The only way we could tip the balance in our favour was by realizing this story is too big for one person. It requires a community to stand with us and believe in the power of a story to change minds, to change behaviours and to change at least some small corner of the world.

I know this story has already impacted at least one life: mine. Sometimes I feel like this story picked me rather than the other way around. I don't always feel qualified or experienced enough to share it. My feelings of inadequacy raise their heads like little monsters, taunting me some days. In one of these moments I told Leor I was feeling apprehensive.

He held me by the shoulders, looked into my eyes and asked, "Why are you doing this?" I thought back to the night prior, when I heard terrible news stories of parents murdering their children and refugees drowning as they tried to escape their war-torn region. It left me feeling hopeless, helpless, in despair.

I looked back at Leor and told him, "I'm sharing this story because it will give people hope. It is a little bit of light amid the darkness."

"That's right," he said. "Don't forget it — you have a purpose that is greater than you and greater than the fear you might feel."

I know he is right. I have been given a second lease on life, and I cannot let it go to waste. I want to be an ambassador for hope and tell stories that will help others like me to remember there is a reason for living and there are others who need our help.

Coming home, I also realized the people of Afghanistan still had more to teach me. I also realized this film is not actually about Afghanistan. It's not even just about women or equality. It is much larger than all of that.

Now that I can finally share this story with others, I've had people tell me they don't always feel safe to walk or run in certain areas of their city or even their own neighbourhoods in the dark. What the people of Bamyan, Afghanistan, are doing is amazing because by creating a safe race they have also created a safe place. What if we could use races to reclaim the spaces where we feel most un-safe here in North America? I'm looking forward to hosting the first race with the Running Room and the charity Canadian Women for Women in Afghanistan to celebrate the message of the film: everyone should be free to run.

I'm still running, inspired by the women I met in Afghanistan and by the people in my new neighbourhood who are part of the Beaches Running Room club in Toronto. Together, I believe if we can keep putting one foot in front of the other we can make sure that every person, regardless of their gender, religion, race or ability, is free to run. I know movement is medicine for me, and I want to make sure that this basic human right to move and be free is extended to all.

During the day, Kate, John, Liz, Leanne and I exchanged reports on how the events went, and we had a debriefing session with the race directors about how everything had gone in their respective cities. We were all thrilled at how successful it had been, the enthusiasm and positivity of all involved, and we were excited at the prospect of repeating the event, on an annual basis. For Autumn, it was a great learning experience that she thoroughly enjoyed. I felt glad about involving her. She too said she wanted to do it all over again. She had had 32 people register and "next time, I want 100!" That's my girl!

Over the following days and weeks, we received photos and videos from all over the world, documenting their Secret Marathon 3K events, including images and videos from Zainab in Afghanistan. Following are some of their voices.

FRIBA REZAYEE – RACE DIRECTOR, VANCOUVER

I was born and raised in Afghanistan. I grew up in the capital, Kabul. As a girl, I never felt safe going outside by myself, especially not for jogging or running. There are many factors that made it difficult for me to feel safe going outside: harassment from many men and boys on the road (because they're not used to seeing girls jog or run on the streets, and unfortunately it is very common for men and boys to harass women and girls because whatever men and boys do, they get away it with because it's a male-dominated society), and family restrictions. Lone girls aren't allowed to go outside without the company of a male family member, for fear that she might begin a love affair with a stranger and start dating (which is highly shameful in the Afghan society), and bring shame to the family.

And last, the majority of families are afraid that girls will become independent, they will develop self-empowerment from sports, girls will get mentally strong, and it will become hard for their family members to control them, especially the male family members. There is a belief that women and girls are the property of male family members, first property of fathers and brothers, and after marriage, the property of their husbands.

There is a famous hill in Kabul called Tap-e-Wazir Akbar Khan. It's famous for being located in the rich neighbourhood of Kabul city, where foreign diplomats, Afghan-famous artists, such as singers or musicians, and many politicians live. It's 20–25 minutes' walking distance from my family home, where I partially grew up (my father still lives there).

I always wanted to go on top of that hill and walk or run, also enjoy the view of the city. But because it wasn't safe or easy for the mentioned reasons, I kept my route and plan secret to avoid comments from both my family and the people outside. Whenever I went on top of the hill, I felt so free and empowered and had a great sense of self-accomplishment, that "Yes, I did it!!!" feeling.

Therefore, I understand the value of participating in The Secret Marathon 3K run/walk in Canada on March 7. I was honoured to fight for the safe space for Afghan girls and women in Afghanistan. Everyone deserves to feel safe when going outside, either for a walk or for exercise; Afghan women have the same rights on the road as Afghan men. My fight for this cause will continue.

Let's normalize girls running in Afghanistan!

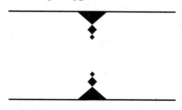

AUTUMN BEYERS (AGE 14)– RACE DIRECTOR, SUDBURY

I participated in the Secret Marathon 3K race because I felt like I needed to help those women and girls to run and make difference in their future. The Secret Marathon 3K taught me a lot about what these girls and women go through, and it meant a lot to me to be able to participate in this run for these strong, courageous girls and women who have a dream that I could help make come true.

JADE AZZARIA –
MOTHER AND WIFE, COCHRANE

Thank you for inspiring my son and husband to run for justice.

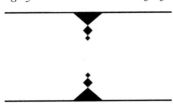

HIELKJE KLOK – PARTICIPANT, CALGARY

My reason for participating in The Secret Marathon 3K was to help raise awareness for the plight of women in Afghanistan as well as women in other countries. As women we need to unite together so that we can be heard for equality for all, no matter which country we live in. What it meant to me to participate is the satisfaction of being able to participate and have our voices heard, so that women all over the world will know that someone is there for support.

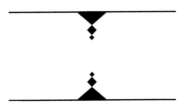

CHARMAINE MONTEIRO – PARTICIPANT, CALGARY

Many thanks for organizing this very worthwhile event. Thank you for bringing awareness to the plight of women in Afghanistan. I ran because I grew up in Pakistan, a country that is known for its violation of women's rights, among other things. I started running at the age of 50 (and love it!). When I read about The Secret

Marathon, it dawned on me that I would not have had the option/choice or opportunity to run if I was still living in Pakistan. That's why I chose to participate.

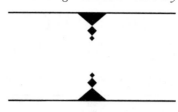

NADA MERHI – PARTICIPANT, CALGARY

Where do I start?! I participated in The Secret Marathon 3K mainly for raising awareness for the cause; to empower women and give them the rights they deserve in today's society. It was a wonderful experience running with fellow change makers in the city I was born and raised in! I have a deep respect for Calgarians. They are the most accepting and kind community. My city is a part of who I am, and I'm very proud of that.

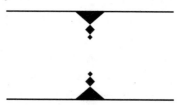

ALISON SCHMIDT – PARTICIPANT, EDMONTON

Sometimes I think Canadians just take our rights and freedom for granted. I need money, so I work. I need food, so I go to the store. I like to run, so I run. The idea that there are places in the world where ordinary women like me can't just tie up their shoes, step out the door and enjoy a physical activity as basic as running is mind-blowing. No one should be prevented from participating in running, or any other activity, because of their gender. Thanks for sponsoring this wonderful event. What a great way to celebrate International Women's Day.

AMY RAWLINSON – PARTICIPANT, EDMONTON

In Edmonton, we ran in an area near the famous Whyte Avenue. We ran along the beautiful river valley, along scenic Saskatchewan Drive. This area is close to the University of Alberta campus; it is a largely popular area for trendy shops and restaurants and is truly a vibrant and sought-after location for many festivals and events throughout the year. Unfortunately, throughout the six years I have lived here, I have heard countless stories of attempted abductions, sexual harassment and assault on women travelling through this area either on their own or in groups of friends. It is an area that is commonly in the news for gang and gun violence, and at night there is often a large police presence. This is truly disheartening, and I was so inspired by the idea brought forward by The Secret Marathon 3K to "reclaim" these spaces and to "reimagine" their intended use as fun, vibrant spaces in which to go out and enjoy the community this area represents.

There was a fantastic turnout of all ages and a true sense of equality shared among all the participants. The Running Room group I belong to in the Callingwood area usually has attendees who express they are a part of the group, so they feel accountable but also to feel a sense of safety while running at night. I think it was great to have a run dedicated to drawing attention to the latter, and I hope to see runs like this continue in various areas within our cities.

Fantastic job to everyone involved in The Secret Marathon 3K! I wish for continued success in your fundraising goals going forward.

MONICA STOROZUK – PARTICIPANT, WINNIPEG

Wow! What a great turnout. Congratulations to you and all the organizers for a wonderful event. I participated in The Secret Marathon 3K because I want to support the women of Afghanistan in their efforts to live full lives free of oppression. The struggle for human rights is universal, and I believe we all need to use our voices and our actions to improve our world. Thank you, and see you next year.

ARIELLA TSAFATINOS – PARTICIPANT, TORONTO

Besides being a professional fitness enthusiast, a regular runner, and a marathon runner when the spirit moves me, I also work every day in my capacity as an adult ESL instructor at the Toronto and District School Board, with women and men from parts of the world where women are not treated equally, Afghanistan included. These newcomers have found their way here to Canada, where they are learning about Canadian values and are enjoying so much more freedom and safety and are incredibly grateful for their good fortune. I feel fortunate as well to have the opportunity to learn about their customs and cultures, and to help them learn English and adapt to their new home.

When I learned of your event, I didn't have to think too hard to get involved. At FitnessWorks for Women, our mission is to empower women to manifest positive changes in their lives, by contributing to women's health and happiness through our unwavering commitment to creating community and to providing intelligent options for their health and fitness. Additionally, Canadians, I think, are quite naturally a caring population, as many are sponsoring families or raising awareness or raising money to help effect positive change in the world, as your film is doing.

Personally, I hope to be able to continue to be a supporter of women and people in general in as many ways as I can, as the ripple effect is far-reaching.

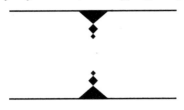

MARIA HOMAYUN – PARTICIPANT, OTTAWA

The cause was very close to my heart as an individual who believes in human rights, and unfortunately, women's rights are not seen as human rights by everyone everywhere. As an Afghan – partaking in the marathon was the least I could do to show support and help in my own little way. It is easy to watch the news and feel helpless, but attending these events makes one realize that other people out there are actively showing support and care for the same cause – and that in itself provides a little bit of relief.

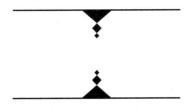

LORI ARMSTRONG – PARTICIPANT, INUVIK

Having lived in many different communities around the world and seen the ways that sexism and gender inequality harm all of us in those communities, I wanted to show my support for a positive expression of solidarity, change and hope, like The Secret Marathon 3K.

SUE ROBINSON – PARTICIPANT, NEW JERSEY, USA

I participated in The Secret Marathon 3K because it's a cause I believe in, and it was a great opportunity to raise awareness of the mission among my friends and network. I understand that individuals standing together in a group can accomplish so much more than one individual standing alone. As a participant in The Secret Marathon, I know I was part of the group that's bringing the very basic freedom of being able to run safely to those for whom it's been denied.

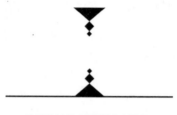

ZAINAB HUSSAINI – PARTICIPANT, MAZAR-E-SHARIF, AFGHANISTAN

We did The Secret Marathon 3K just today at 6:30 a.m. because of the security; we had lots of fun, a powerful message for our community. I hope this kind of movement helps all of us fight for equality!

The motto for The Secret Marathon 3K was: Running, Walking and Working Together for Equality. This is just the beginning. At this writing, plans are already under way for the Second Secret Marathon 3K, on Wednesday, March 6, 2019.

AFTERWORD

The First Secret Marathon 3K was a huge success, and the event registrations raised over $6,000 for the film. This was very timely, as raising funds to make the film was proving to be a real challenge. In September 2016, Viiz had stepped up with $25,000, which allowed us to shoot the film in Afghanistan. However, funds were still needed for all the post-production costs, including editing, music, sound mixing and so on. During 2017, Kate, Scott and I had explored several avenues for raising money, with limited success. These included participating in the Field Law Community Fund online competition for $30,000 (we didn't win), approaching the National Film Board of Canada, CBC and Telus (some interest but no money) and applying for various grants (no luck).

I came to realize that it takes a lot of work to get a film made, no matter how much you believe in it. However, even though we had had some failures at raising funds, we also had some successes. Kate secured a grant for $3,000 from Ryerson University, and she and Scott set up a crowd-funding page. By late March 2018 we had hit our $15,000 target. This was made up of donations ranging from $10 to $100 from individuals who believed in the project. John and James from Viiz stepped forward, yet again, with $10,000 to cover the cost of original music and sound mix.

The plan was to have the film finished by mid-May 2018 and submit it to film festivals both national and international. We agreed that the premier should be at the Toronto International Film Festival, held in early

September 2018, and in order to qualify it had to be submitted, at the latest, by June 1. By late April, Scott had completed the rough cut and we wanted to get feedback from Kubra, Zainab, Mahsa and Nelofar before we went any further. I sent out the film and got positive comments from three of the women. However, on April 8, Nelofar sent me this email:

Hi Martin,

Hope you are well! Sorry if this sounds negative but please remove all my details including video, pictures and whatever, but if you want you can include only my name by text but not anything of picture or video. I am under threat because of my activities more than [at] that time, and I believe this film can make it worse than ever. I can't explain what kind of threat but just want to request that please do whatever I have mentioned above. Else you know my life is in danger and as a pro[of], please kindly reply to me that you will do these all.

Best,

Nelofar

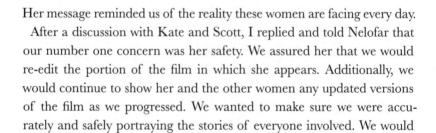

Her message reminded us of the reality these women are facing every day.

After a discussion with Kate and Scott, I replied and told Nelofar that our number one concern was her safety. We assured her that we would re-edit the portion of the film in which she appears. Additionally, we would continue to show her and the other women any updated versions of the film as we progressed. We wanted to make sure we were accurately and safely portraying the stories of everyone involved. We would also review all social-media posts and remove references to her wherever possible. I asked her to please let us know if we could help her in any other way.

This turn of events changed everything. We removed Nelofar from the film. This took more time in the editing process, and consequently meant we would not be able to complete the film in time for the 2018 film-festival circuit. At this writing, the plan is to submit the film in 2019.

My training and race season for "62 Beats 47" continues. At this writing, I have completed four races: Airdrie 5K, Calgary 5K, Sporting Life 10K and MEC 10K. So far, no personal bests have been broken, but my times are improving. I still have five races to go: Edmonton Half-Marathon, Dino Dash 10K, 2018 Marathon of Afghanistan, Last Chance half-marathon and the California International Marathon in Sacramento in December. Fingers crossed.

And yes, you read that correctly. I am registered in the Marathon of Afghanistan for 2018. It's early August as I write this, and my preparations are moving head for the Afghanistan race in October. My flights are booked and now it's time to apply for the visa. Checking on the website for the Ottawa-based Embassy of Afghanistan, there are a few extra requirements on the application this year. Hopefully, the lessons I learned from last time will put me in good stead to get the visa with more than five hours to spare.

I've been in touch with Stephanie and Taylor at Free to Run about my visit in October and, with my annual year-end fundraiser in mind, I asked what future projects they were planning. They told me they have applied for a grant to support the girls and women to learn to play ice hockey. I'm looking forward to having discussions with them to see how the Ninth Annual Run/Walk can support this initiative.

I'm very excited about heading back to Bamyan and running the marathon. The highlight will be to run with three of the women who participated in the 2016 Marathon of Afghanistan: Kubra, Nelofar and Mahsa, as well as with one who didn't run that year.

Zainab inspired me as I was recovering from a clot on the brain. Her strength and courage to keep running in the face of adversity made me want to go to Afghanistan and support the women and girls. She couldn't run in the 2016 event but is planning to run, with her husband, in the 2018 race.

The story has come full circle, but the journey continues.

ACKNOWLEDGEMENTS

My trip to Afghanistan introduced me to a group of strong, fearless females who are making a difference. The chapters contributed to the book by these women and girls are powerful, moving and raw. Thank you, Zainab, Kubra, Nelofar, Mahsa, Behishta and Zahra. These girls and women have taken great personal risk by telling their stories.

I also want to thank the following event organizers and Free to Run representatives who were at the start line of the Marathon of Afghanistan at 8:00 a.m. on November 4, 2016, and have contributed their stories, in their own words: James Willcox, James Bingham, Taylor Smith and Connie Schneider.

Preparations for the trip were fraught with challenges and misgivings. Two people living in Cochrane helped me along the way. My family physician, Doctor Bill Hanlon, has worked extensively in Afghanistan and guided me on health and security issues. Chris Shank was project manager in developing Band-e Amir National Park and gave me invaluable local knowledge about Bamyan Province. On top of that, Chris, working with his contacts in Kabul, facilitated the visa process that ensured my passport, with visa, arrived five hours before my departure time.

Many other people shared the journey. Kate McKenzie, co-director of the film and first-time marathon runner, had the vision and persistence to take this spark of an idea and turn it into a documentary film that will be shared with the world. Scott Townend, co-director of *The Secret Marathon* documentary, was supportive through thick and thin. Colin Scheyen and Liam Kearney were the camera crew that captured the 11 days in Afghanistan.

Jason Webb of Downunder Travel sponsored my flights to and from Kabul.

John Wilson and James MacKenzie of Viiz Communications believed in the cause and sponsored the film.

John Stanton, founder of the Running Room organization, believed in our cause and provided amazing support, enabling us to stage The Secret Marathon 3K run/walk.

Other individuals, groups and sponsors that have helped me on this journey include: Leanne Brintnell and Gitti Sherzad from the Canadian Women for Women in Afghanistan; my running coach, Malc Kent; my TEDx coach, Kam Parel-Nuttall; the Rotary Club of Cochrane; Scotia Calgary Marathon Association; Patsy's Place; Ink'd Graphics; the *Cochrane Times* and the *Cochrane Eagle*.

Thank you, Don Gorman and Jillian van der Geest at Rocky Mountain Books, and my editor, Meaghan Craven, who again turned a simple story into an amazing book.

Finally, I want to thank our sons, Kyle and Calum, for cheering me on from afar, and the strong and fearless women in my life: granddaughter Autumn, who is a chip off the old block and will be pushing me in my future races; daughter Kristina, who, with grandsons Nathan and Matthew Conner, always send notes of support; and my wife, Sue, who has seen it all and is always there at the end of the day to give me a big hug.

ABOUT THE AUTHOR

Martin Parnell is the bestselling author of *Marathon Quest* and *Running to the Edge* and speaks about having a "Finish the Race Attitude" – overcoming obstacles to achieve your full potential. Martin has written for, or been covered by, BBC, CBC, CNN, *Huffington Post, The Globe and Mail, National Post, Runner's World, Men's Journal, Canadian Business* and *Maclean's.*

In a five-year period, from 2010 to 2014, Martin completed ten extreme endurance "quests," including running 250 marathons in one year and raising $1.3-million for the humanitarian organization Right To Play. His TEDx talk, "Life Is a Relay," can be found on YouTube.

Martin is a member of the Rotary Club of Cochrane, Alberta, where he lives with his wife, Sue. They have three children, Kyle, Calum and Kristina, and three grandchildren, Autumn, Nathan and Matthew Connor. Sue and Martin enjoy walking, snowshoeing and tennis. Martin can often be seen running the pathways along the Bow River near their home.

Visit www.martinparnell.com
Contact Martin at info@martinparnell.com
Or call him at 403-922-0562